The Renaissance Imagination

Important Literary and Theatrical Texts
from the Late Middle Ages through
the Seventeenth Century

Stephen Orgel, Editor

A Garland Series

A Critical Edition of
The True Chronicle History of King Leir And His Three Daughters, Gonorill, Ragan and Cordella

Donald M. Michie

GARLAND PUBLISHING, INC.
New York & London
1991

Copyright © 1991 by Donald M. Michie
All Rights Reserved

Library of Congress Cataloging-in-Publication Data

King Leir.
A Critical edition of The true chronicle history of King Leir and his three daughters, Gonorill, Ragan, and Cordella /
[edited by] Donald M. Michie.
p. cm. — (The Renaissance imagination)
Originally presented as the author's thesis
(Ph. D.—University of Wisconsin—Madison).
Includes bibliographical references.
ISBN 0-8153-0456-0 (alk. paper)
1. Lear, King (Legendary character)—Drama. I. Michie, Donald M.
II. Title. III. Title: True chronicle history of King Leir and his three daughters, Gonorill, Ragan, and Cordella. IV. Series: Renaissance imagination (Unnumbered)
PR2411.K55 1991
822'.3—dc20
91-31663

Printed on acid-free, 250-year-life paper
Manufactured in the United States of America

For

Mary Alyce, Michael

and Amy

Acknowledgements

My thanks are due to Professor Standish Henning, my dissertation advisor, for his constructive guidance and his generous support in the development of this thesis and for the time, the effort, and the patience he has shown in the whole process.

I also wish to thank the other members of my committee, Professors Robert Kimbrough, Richard Knowles, and Michael MacDonald, for their critical insights and helpful comments.

CONTENTS

INTRODUCTION 3-55

    I.   Date of First Performance 4

    II.   Date of Publication .4

    III.   The Text 6

    IV.   The Copy for the 1605 Quarto 14

    V.   Sources 18

    VI.   Relationship of *King Leir* to Shakespeare's Play . . . 21

    VII.   A Critical Reading 35

    VIII.   Modern Editions 51

    IX.   Editorial Procedures 52

THE TRUE CHRONICLE HISTORY OF KING LEIR 64-200

BIBLIOGRAPHY: A List of Works Cited 238-244

Introduction

The story of an old man who divides his property among his daughters in reward for their profession of love, and then suffers because he misinterpreted their assurances, is a folk-tale that has been told for centuries throughout Europe and Asia. There are many ancient stories in India about filial ingratitude, "the contrast between good and bad children's treatment of aged parents." [1] In Europe the love-test appears in the story of the Goosegirl-Princess who told her father she "loved him like salt." According to Wilfrid Perrett, [2] there are at least twenty-six variants of the European story in which King Lear suffers at the hands of his two ungrateful daughters. But not until the 1590's was the story dramatized by an anonymous playwright in *The True Chronicle Historie of King Leir and his three daughters*. This dramatist followed the original of the story. Leir uses the love-test to see which of his three daughters loves him best, and later suffers disillusionment after discovering his older daughters' visciousness once they have gained their inheritance. Aided by his close friend Perillus, Leir is restored to his faithful daughter Cordella who with her husband (the king of France) helps Leir regain his throne. The play ends happily; evil is overcome and virtue is rewarded. After its few performances, the play would probably have faded into obscurity if Shakespeare had not used it as one of the major sources for his tragedy *King Lear*. Shakespeare's indebtness to *The True Chronicle Historie* and the fame of his *King Lear* have assured the old play a place of importance in literary study.

I. THE DATE OF ITS FIRST PERFORMANCE

Although we are not sure when *King Leir* was composed (Alfred Harbage and S. Schoenbaum record the play as having been written any time between 1588 and 1594), [3] we do know when it first appeared on stage. Philip Henslowe notes in his Diary that on the sixth and again on the eighth of April, 1594, [4] the play which he calls "king leare" was performed at the Rose Theatre by the "Quenes men and my lord of Susexe to geather." [5] They gave eight performances, and the play was entered in the Stationers' Register on May 15, 1594, as follows:

> Edward White   Entred| alsoe for his Copie vnder th[e h] andes of bothe the wardens a booke entituled|*The moste famous Chronicle historye of LEIRE kinge of England and his three daughters* . . . . vjdC. [6]

The 'C.' after the sum is apparently the initial of the senior warden of the company, Gabriel Cawood, and was perhaps appended in receipt of the fee. [7] No copy of *King Leir* has been found corresponding to the date of the 1594 entry in the Register. In fact, there is no evidence that the play was ever printed as a result of the entry. [8]

II. THE DATE OF PUBLICATION

Eleven years later, on May 8, 1605, the following entry appeared in the Register:

> Simon Stafford   Entered for his Copie vnder th [e h] andes of the Wardens A booke called '*the Tragecall historie of kinge LEIR and his Three Daughters &c.*' As it was Latlie Acted.

Just beneath this entry is the following note:

> John Wright   Enterd for his Copie by assignment from Simon Stafford and by consent of Master Leake, *The Tragicall history of kinge Leire and his Three Daughters* / PROVIDED that Simon Stafford shall haue the printinge of this book.

W. W. Greg discusses this transaction, pointing out that the presence of William Leake's name as the warden authorizing the transfer in 1605, and the entries themselves in the Stationers' Register "are sufficient evidence that no edition had followed the entrance of 1594." For if there had been one, it would presumably have been known: "an honest holder of the copy would not have entered it anew, he would have obtained an assignment; while a pirate would have stood to gain nothing by advertising his theft." [9] This transaction indicates that Simon Stafford transferred to John Wright "not necessarily the recognized ownership of the property in question . . . but only whatever right or claim Stafford might have to it," [10] for the White family held the copyright of *King Leir* until 1624. [11]

John Wright published the play with the following title:

> THE | True Chronicle Hi- | story of King LEIR, and his three | *daughters*, *Gonorill*, *Ragan*, | and *Cordella*. As it hath bene diuers and sundry | times lately acted. | |ornament| LONDON, | Printed by Simon Stafford for Iohn | Wright, and are to bee sold at his shop at | Christes Church dore, next Newgate- | Market. 1605.

King Leir was the first book entered to Wright in the Stationers' Register, assigned to him by Stafford in May, 1605. Because Wright had been White's apprentice, many early critics believed that Wright had stolen the play from his old master. They assumed that since Wright had access to the play and since Shakespeare's *Lear* was a popular play on stage in early 1605, Wright saw an opportunity to make a quick profit for himself. Edmund Malone in 1793 asserted that the 1605 publication of *Leir* was clearly made for the purpose of "palming off" the 1594 play as Shakespeare's. [12] Many critics in the nineteenth century agreed with Malone; among them are John P. Collier, Henry N. Hudson, Alexander Dyce, and Frederick Fleay. [13]

W. W. Greg argues, however, that these early critics, because of their unfamiliarity with the procedures of the Stationers' Company, have naturally put a "sinister interpretation" on the facts related to the play's publication. He points out, first of all, that there is no basis whatsoever for believing that Wright stole the copy from his former master. "If this had been stolen from another stationer, it is unlikely that the publisher would have risked entering it in the Register or would have put his name and address on the edition he issued." Furthermore, "the title page, not the entry, would be the medium for bamboozling the public." [14] It is also clear from the entry that it was Stafford who obtained the copy, not Wright. Wright's association with the printing and publishing of *King Leir* may, therefore, have been mere coincidence or it may have been the result of a friendly negotiation between the master, White, his former apprentice, Wright, and the third party, Simon Stafford.

III. THE TEXT

There are only four known copies of Q, and one of these is imperfect. The three perfect copies are in the British Museum, the Folger Library, and the Huntington Library. The British Museum copy, though perfect, is slightly cropped. The imperfect copy with two leaves missing (C2, C3) is also in the British Museum. It was acquired from J. O. Halliwell-Phillips along with eighteen other rare volumes in a large purchase in 1858, all for the sum of one thousand pounds.[15] The pages of the imperfect copy are supplied in a fine Victorian hand.

King Leir is a book of thirty-six unnumbered leaves. It collates A-I4. A1 is the title page, A1v is blank, A2 bears the head title. The text beginning on A2 is completed on I4v. All leaves are signed. The speech prefixes are indented; they and the stage directions are set in italics. Entrance directions are usually centered, and exits and other directions are placed in the margin. Catchwords appear regularly on the signature line; there are no anomalies.

The running head title "The History of King Leir and his three daughters" is repeated at the top of each opening. Variations in the type setting of the titles may be shown as follows:

A1	-	TP	A1v	-	BLANK	D1	-	III	D1v	-	V
A2v	-	I	A2	-	HT	D2v	-	II	D2	-	IV
A3	-	III	A3v	-	I	D3	-	IV	D3v	-	II
A4v	-	V	A4	-	I	D4v	-	V	D4	-	III
B1	-	VI	B1v	-	II	E1	-	III	E1v	-	VII
B2v	-	V	B2	-	III	E2v	-	I	E2	-	VIII
B3	-	IV	B3v	-	V	E3	-	VIII	E3v	-	II
B4v	-	II	B4	-	VI	E4v	-	V	E4	-	III
C1	-	III	C1v	-	I	F1	-	III	F1v	-	I
C2v	-	I	C2	-	III	F2v	-	I	F2	-	III
C3	-	VI	C3v	-	V	F3	-	VIII	F3v	-	V
C4v	-	V	C4	-	VI	F4v	-	V	F4	-	VIII
G1	-	VIII	G1	-	VII	I1	-	VIII	I1v	-	VII
G2v	-	VII	G2	-	VIII	I2v	-	VII	I2	-	VIII
G3	-	III	G3v	-	II	I3	-	III	I3v	-	II
G4v	-	II	G4	-	III	I4v	-	II	I4	-	III
H1	-	III	H1v	-	I						
H2v	-	I	H2	-	III						
H3	-	VIII	H3v	-	V						
H4v	-	V	H4	-	VIII						

Sheets A through G have 38 lines per page (D3v being an exception with only 37). Sheet H has 39 lines per page; and sheet I has 39 except I3v with 38 lines and I4v with 35 lines. Apparently as a compositor approached the end of the text, he saw that he could complete the text within the last two sheets, H and I, so that he would not have to compose another page on what would have been sheet K. He completed the text on I4v within 35 lines, but if the extra line had not been added to each of the eight pages of sheet H and to each of the six pages of sheet I, then the compositor would have had eight to ten lines to compose on the next sheet K. By adding the extra line to sheets H and I, he avoided the expense of paper and the time needed for setting another forme.

We can infer that the text, or at least parts of the text, was composed by formes rather than seriatim. [16] One indication of this is the pattern of italic I substitutions during the composition of the text. Sheet D exhibits a shortage of the roman I in signatures D2, D3v, and D4. At no time in the sheets preceding D has a compositor used the italic I in the text proper, and the compositor setting sheet D was apparently not indifferent to the I/*I* distinction. It appears that he used the proper character until his supply was nearly exhausted. If he were setting the sheet consecutively, there would be little reason for him to substitute italic I's on signature D2 and then to skip down to signatures D3v and D4 before substituting the italic I's again (see Table A below). We can theorize that the compositor was setting by formes rather than consecutively, for he had a sufficient supply of the roman character as he set the outer forme of sheet D, but he lacked the right amount of roman I's as he set the inner forme of sheet D. In composing signatures D2, D3v, and D4, he had to substitute the italic I. An order of setting in which D2, D3v, and D4 are set at one time and in which D1, D2v, D3, and D4v are set at another time is comprehensible only if we assume that the compositor was setting by formes rather than setting consecutively.

Table A: Evidence for Setting by Formes

The grouping of italic I's if set consecutively:									The groupings of italic I's if set by formes:							
	D1	1v	2	2v	3	3v	4	4v	D1	2v	3	4v	1v	2	3v	4
I	8	16	3	9	16	4	4	11	8	9	13	11	16	3	4	4
I	0	0	13	0	0	5	20	0	0	0	0	0	0	13	5	20

This rearrangement by formes reveals a sufficiency of the roman I character for all the pages of the outer forme and for the first page of the inner forme.

Another indication that the text was set by formes is in the squeezed typography on sheet I. The speakers on I2 (inner forme) and I2v (outer forme) are engaged in one line repartee. However, the type on I2 is very closely set: the single lines of the individual speakers and their speech prefixes are set consecutively without regard for providing an indentation for each speaker. But this is not the case in I2v. There is no crowding on the typography; each speech is set in separate paragraphs. The compositor presumably composed the outer forme first, [17] but in composing the inner forme he discovered that he had more lines to set than he had room for. That accounts for the excessive crowding of lines on that page.

There were probably three compositors at work on the composition of *King Leir*. Each compositor is distinguished by the distinct differences in his use of speech-prefix forms and in his spelling preferences [18] (see Table B) One compositor (compositor X) set sheets A-B, another (compositor Y) set sheets C and E-I, and another (compositor Z) set sheet D. Compositor Y clearly prefers the speech prefix *King*. over the abbreviated form, *Kin*. He uses *King*. 41 times on sheets C and E-1. He also uses only the *Mes*. form for messenger 46 times rather than the *Mess*. form favored by compositor Z. Compositor Y also uses prefers the *Cor*. prefix for Cordella, using it 38 times, although he tolerates the *Cord*. form, employing it 9 times. Compositor Z, setting sheet D, prefers the prefix *Kin*., using it nine times. He also prefers the *Mess*. abbreviation on that sheet. The prefix for Cordella does not appear on his sheet. As far as spelling preferences, both compositors Y and Z prefer the do/go spellings over the doe/goe spellings, although an occasional doe/goe spelling occurs on sheets C, E-I. In contrast, compositor Y uses only the do/go spelling from F (outer forme) on to the end of the text. Compositor Z, who set sheet D, seems to prefer the Oh spelling, using it three times. However, that is hardly enough data to confirm his preference for that form. Compositor Y prefers the O spelling using it 30 times, but tolerates the Oh spelling using it 18 times.

The third compositor (compositor X) differs from Y and Z in his indifference to various forms of spelling and speech prefixes. On sheets A and B, he prefers the do/go spellings, using them 15 times on sheet A and 14 times on sheet B. However, he tolerates doe/goe spellings, using them three times on sheet A and seven times on sheet B. In contrast to compositor Z, he prefers the O spelling, using it three times. He is indifferent to the use of *King./Kin.*, *Cord./Cor.*, and *Rag./Ra.* prefixes, using them almost equally. The *Mes./Mess.* forms do not appear on sheets A and B. Therefore, what distinguishes him from the other two compositors is his seeming lack of concern most of the time as to which forms of words he uses as he sets the type.

Table B

Speech-prefixes	Compositors:	X	Y	Z
	Sheets:	(A-B)	(C,E-I)	(D)
Kin./King		2/2	0/41	9/0
Mes./Mess.		---	46/0	0/4
Cor./Cord		3/4	38/9	---
Ra./Rag.		9/9	9/22	0/1
Spellings				
do,go/doe,goe		29/10	110/4	14/2
O/Oh		3/0	38/18	0/3

King Leir is a cleanly printed play with a minimal number of editorial problems. There are, however, at least two problems which require some exploration and explanation. One of them is to be inferred from sheet D (inner forme) and signature E4v of the text. Apparently, a shortage of the roman I forced the compositor to substitute the italic I on these pages until his supply of the roman font was replenished. Secondly, on sheet F (outer forme) an indiscriminate mixing of the roman I's with italic I's occurs, a mixing which continues to the end of the text. The italic I had been used as a substitute form on D2, D3v, D4, and on E4v, because the line of demarcation between the italic I and the roman I on these pages is distinct. But that is not the case from sheet F (outer forme) onward. There, the mixing is indiscriminate (see Table C). There is, however, some explanation for these two problems.

We first consider the substitution of the italic for roman font on sheet D. We assume that sheet A and perhaps one of the formes for sheet B derived their supply of roman I's from initially full cases and from distribution of earlier press work. And as work progressed, the compositors distributed the wrought off formes as soon as they were through the press. According to Professor Robert K. Turner, this was probably standard procedure: a compositor, "working on the assumption that composition and presswork could stay more or less in balance, "attempted "to follow the conventional procedure for setting by formes--to compose two formes, distribute the first, set the third, distribute the second, and so on." [19] This procedure holds true whether for one-skeleton printing or for two or more skeleton printings. [20] One skeleton printing was used throughout most of the text of *King Leir* because one head title (III) appears on nearly every forme, inner and outer. Other running titles do not appear with the regularity of III; but like III, some appear on both inner and outer formes of the same sheet. This regularity is a clear indication of one skeleton printing. If the compositors of *King Leir* were following the procedure outlined by Turner, then while outer forme of A was being machined, the inner forme of A would be distributed, and inner forme of B would be composed. Subsequently, when sheets C and D were being worked on, the inner forme of C should have been distributed, either before or while the inner forme of D was being composed, assuming that the inner forme preceded outer forme both in setting and in printing. Professor Turner also points out that "ideally one forme ought to be machined in the time required to distribute the immediately preceding forme and to set and impose the next." [21] Therefore, in an ideal situation, one in which the compositors and pressmen show a "fine consideration for timing," we could expect that the procedures outlined by Turner would have been followed. Let us assume that the compositors adhered to this procedure, at least in the setting of the first three sheets of the text. As long as the compositors and the pressmen were working efficiently, there was little chance for the compositor to run short of any font, and until it was time to compose sheet D (inner forme), the compositors had plenty of roman I's.

However, sheet C had required an inordinate number of roman I's (95 pieces). In the procedure outlined by Turner, the inner forme of C should have been distributed and the inner forme of D composed while the outer forme of C was being machined. But let us assume that for some reason the inner forme of C was not distributed as it normally would have been. Consequently, the three formes--sheet C (inner forme) with 63 pieces and C (outer forme) being machined with 32 pieces, and D (inner forme) which needed a total of 65 pieces for setting--all put a strain on the roman I supply. The total number of I's at this point either in the press or ready for distribution or needed for composing was 160 pieces--an extraordinarily high number of upper case I's in comparison to the demands being made on other upper case letters. So as the new compositor (Z) began the composition of D (inner forme), he had approximately 20 roman I's, but he needed 65 pieces. We are assuming that Z worked from Y's case; if Z has composed from his own, he would probably have had enough roman I's. After using 16 pieces on page D1v, he began substituting the italic case on page D2 when he saw that his stock of roman I's was low. [22] The line of demarcation between the two fonts is distinct. On pages D3v and D4, eight more roman I's appear, mixed in no particular order on those pages with the italic I's. There is a possible explanation for this mixing: the compositor may in the course of setting have discovered some more roman I's that he had earlier overlooked and then inserted them as he composed, a possibility suggested by some of George Williams' work on various texts cited above.

On the next sheet, sheet E, a new compositor (Y) set the inner forme after a distribution had been made, only to run out of roman I's after setting 85 on E4v (outer forme). At that point, he set his last seven roman I's before he began the substitution of the italic. The dividing line between the two fonts is as clear here as it was on D2; nevertheless, a stray roman I appears later on that page mixed with the italics. It appears that both compositors (compositor Z on sheet D and compositor Y on sheet E), working from the same case, used up what they thought were the last of the roman letters before they began setting with the italics.

The second problem with the compositors' use of italic I occurs on sheet F (outer forme) where an indiscriminate mixing of roman I's occurs, and that mixing continues to the end of the text. After compositor Y had composed sheet E and before he began composing sheet F (inner forme), more type was distributed so that the inner forme of sheet F is free of the italic I. After this, the type from earlier presswork on sheet D was probably distributed and the cases were restocked. [23] However, it appears that the italic I's substituted by compositor Z on sheet D (inner forme) were inadvertently distributed to the roman I case, perhaps by another compositor or an apprentice unaware that the substitution had taken place as sheet D was composed, for from F (outer form) on the the end of the text, the italic and roman I's are mixed indiscriminately on each sheet. The declining ratio of italic letters to roman letters on sheets F-1 offers some substantiation for this theory. The ratio of italic letters to roman letters quite naturally diminishes toward the end of the text, an indication that, as work progressed and other formes from earlier press-work were distributed and the cases re-stocked, the compositor's chances of drawing out an italic I became less and less. Therefore, by the time sheet I was composed, only six italic I's appear on a sheet that had 62 roman I's. The heavy concentration of roman I's on some pages and italic I's on others can perhaps be explained in this manner: as distribution from earlier press-work took place, the roman and italic letters, although missorted, were nevertheless clustered together from time to time, and the compositor would inadvertently draw from those high concentrations of fonts as he composed.

Table C: The Compositor's Substitutions
of Italic I's for Roman I's

	A1	*2v*	*3*	*4v*	*1v*	*2*	*3v*	*4*		*B1*	*2v*	*3*	*4v*	*1v*	*2*	*3v*	*4*
I		4	9	7		4	6	13		9	14	14	12	11	12	13	13
I		0	0	0		0	0	0		0	0	0	0	0	0	0	0

	C1	*2v*	*3*	*4v*	*1v*	*2*	*3v*	*4*		*D1*	*2v*	*3*	*4v*	*1v*	*2*	*3v*	*4*
I		8	4	10	10	14	17	18	14	8	9	16	11	16	3	4	4
I		0	0	0	0	0	0	0	0	0	0	0	0	0	13	5	20

	E1	*2v*	*3*	*4v*	*1v*	*2*	*3v*	*4*		*F1*	*2v*	*3*	*4v*	*1v*	*2*	*3v*	*4*
I		8	6	22	8	10	12	11	8	10	18	10	1	10	12	15	15
I		0	0	0	9	0	0	0	0	4	0	4	7	0	0	0	0

	G1	2v	3	4v	1v	2	3v	4		H1	2v	3	4v	1v	2	3v	4
I	9	5	7	11	6	15	6	9		5	6	14	8	3	17	2	6
I	4	2	5	0	7	3	1	2		2	0	4	4	0	1	1	2

	I1	2v	3	4v	1v	2	3v	4
I	10	3	8	13	3	17	2	6
I	1	1	0	0	0	1	1	2

IV. THE COPY FOR THE 1605 QUARTO

We must ask what sort of copy was handed to the printer in 1605 to provide him with the basis for the quarto. In an earlier discussion we concluded that an edition of the play probably did not appear soon after the entry in the Stationers' Register in 1594. Greg points out that a holder of the copy would not have re-entered it nor would a pirate have gained anything by advertising his theft; furthermore, the warden William Leake authorized the transfer in 1605. Greg's interpretation of all this evidence in the Register is that there is little possibility that the play was published in 1594. [24] Assuming then that the printer in 1605 did not set the text from an earlier printed version, we must then decide what sort of manuscript he used: the author's foul papers or his fair copy; or a playhouse prompt book which in turn may have been foul papers or fair copy that had been altered by the bookkeeper in the preparation and production of the drama. A great deal may have happened to the text between 1594 and its publication (assuming that these are the same plays), but there is "no clear internal evidence of much alteration." [25]

Wilfred Jewkes claims that an author's manuscript probably was the copy for the quarto of *King Leir*. "There is no clear evidence of preparation by a stage revisor or prompter, and it seems probable that an author's manuscript . . . formed the copy for the play." [26] R. B. McKerrow in "The Elizabethan Printer and Dramatic Manuscripts" [27] and W. W. Greg in *The Shakespeare First Folio* [28] have outlined and discussed the distinction that can be made between a text that is based on an author's manuscript (whether foul papers or fair copy) and one that is based on a prompt-book. [29] The focus of their discussions is on the different forms of stage directions that are characteristic of the author on the one hand and of the book-keeper on the other. Stage directions written by the playwright are, in general, different from those inserted by the book-keeper who prepares the play for performance. According to Greg, a playwright's stage directions are descriptive and are of little use to the prompter. They describe a scene as the author conceived it while writing, and they have an "evocative quality" as though they were written for the reader rather than for the actor. A stage direction from Shakespeare's *3 Henry VI* illustrates this point: *Enter a Sonne that hath kill'd his Father, at one dorre: and a Father that hath kill'd his Sonne at another dorre* (II.v.55). This stage direction has that "evocative quality" Greg speaks of; it explains the situation and sets the tone for the speeches that follow. It is, therefore, of "no immediate help to the prompter," but describes a scene as the author imagined it while writing, "and which could at best . . . serve the company in the production of the play." [30] The prompter would in all likelihood not have written it.

A few of Greg's classes of authorial directions are listed below, followed by stage directions from *King Leir* (Q spelling) to illustrate each class:

1. Characters described on their first appearance, their status and relationships defined:

(Scene 30) *Enter the Gallian King . . . and souldiers, with the chiefe of the towne bound.*

2. Action accompanying or following the entrance of actors:

(Scene 14) *Enter the Prince of Cambria, Ragan and Nobles: looke upon them, and whisper together.*

(Scene 19) *See them and start.*

(Scene 31) *Sound Alarum: excursions. Mumford must chase Cambria away: then cease. Enter Cornwal.*

3. Reason or occasion of their appearance explained:

(Scene 12) *Enter the Messenger that should go to Cambria, with a letter in his hand.*

4. Habits and disguises noted:

(Scene 5) *Enter the King of Cornwall and his man booted and spurd, a riding wand, and a letter in his hand.*

(Scene 7) *Enter Gallian King, and Mumford, disguised like pilgrims.*

(Scene 23) *Enter Leir, Perillus, and two Mariners, in sea-gowns and sea-caps.*

(Scene 24) *Enter Gallian King and Queene, and Mumford, with a basket, disguised like countrey folks.*

5. Expressions, mental conditions noted:

(Scene 15) *She reads the letter, frownes and stamps.*

6. Independent actions described:

(Scene 5) *Then they draw lots.*

(Scene 10) *He weeps.*

(Scene 12) *Flings him a purse.*

(Scene 12) *She opens them.*

(Scene 14) *She runneth to him, and kneels down, saying.*

7. Properties required.

(Scene 5) *. . . a riding wand, and a letter.*

(Scene 12) *. . . a letter in his hand.*

(Scene 17) *Give him two purses.*

(Scene 19) *. . . murtherer with two daggers . . . ; Shew their Bookes; Shew a bagge of money.*

(Scene 23) *. . . sea-gowns and sea-caps; Pull off Perillus cloke.*

>(Scene 24) . . . *with a basket; She bringeth him to the table; Perillus proffers his dublet.*
>
>(Scene 29) *Enter the watchmen drunke, with each a pot.*

8. Noises of all sorts:

>(Scene 19) *Thunder and lightning; it thunders.*
>
>(Scene 26) *Sound drum & Trumpets.*
>
>(Scene 28) . . . *a still march.*
>
>(Scene 29) *Alarum . . . ; Alarums and excursions, then sound victory; sound Drummes and Trumpets.*

Stage directions written by the book-keeper are different from those of the author. In considering the language used for stage directions, A. W. Pollard in *Shakespeare's Fight With the Pirates* argued that characteristic prompter's notes are usually written in the imperative mood while the author writes directions in the indicative; therefore, when a number of notes are written in the imperative, then the printed quarto has a prompt copy behind it.[31] W.W. Greg, however, points out that most dramatists were men of the theatre and would use the language of the stage in their stage directions as readily as would the prompter when he made his notes.[32] *King Leir* has many directions that could be cited as characteristic of the prompter if we follow Pollard's theory: *"kisse the paper,"* xii.108; *"Give him two purses,"* xvii.72; and *"draw to stab them,"* xxix.17. However, there are just as many stage directions written in the indicative mood; furthermore, directions in both moods often appear on the same page. Although it is possible that the prompter added the imperative directions to the manuscript, their presence is still not strong evidence in support of the prompt copy as the source of the quarto. In his argument against assuming that the language of the prompter will be different from that of the dramatist, Greg points out that "there is hardly a stage direction that can be cited as characteristic of the prompter that cannot be paralleled from texts for which the author was probably alone responsible."[33] There are, however, other characteristics that are more reliable in assessing whether a prompt copy was the basis for the text.

According to R.B. McKerrow, many stage directions in the printed text of a play will have certain unmistakable characteristics if the text has a playhouse prompt-book as its source. One characteristic is "warnings, either of actors who are to be ready for entry, or of properties which are required for use later." An author would be concerned with stage properties but not with warnings or items to be made ready for use later in the scene. On the other hand, the prompter would make a note of these kinds of details in the prompt book; such provisions would be essential to his carrying out his duties. Another characteristic of the prompt-book is the mention of an actor's name as a gloss, for in a prompt copy the actor's name "always appears *in addition* to the name of the character, not substituted for it." Finally, another characteristic is "the entry of characters before the proper time": what was intended by the prompter as a warning for the actors to be ready to enter has been printed by the printer as an actual entrance. [34] Since these are the distinguishing marks of a text based upon a prompt book we must assume that if any one or all these characteristics are present in the quarto of *King Leir*, we can be reasonably assured that it had as its source the book-keeper's prompt copy. However, none of these traits are present in the quarto. There is no clear evidence of the prompter's hand in the text. All of this evidence on the kinds of stage directions in the quarto of *King Leir* suggests that the author's manuscript, most likely his fair copy, formed the basis for the 1605 text. We cannot, however, be absolutely sure of that. It is quite possible that a literary scribe tidied up the author's rough copy, or he may have removed the marks of stage adaptation from the prompt-book before the manuscript went to the printer. Whatever the case, it nevertheless appears that the text of *King Leir* was based on a very clean copy.

V. SOURCES

The Lear story, a tale with the love-test and filial ingratitude as its prominent features, first appears in England with Geoffrey of Monmouth's *Historia regium Britanniae* (c. 1135) in which Lear is the tenth king to rule in a line from Brut. Geoffrey Bullough points out that the widespread diffusion of

Monmouth's *Historia* in England and on the Continent made the story of Lear well known for several centuries. The *Historia* became quite popular at the end of the fifteenth century in England when Henry VII appointed a commission to trace Tudor ancestry.[35]

Wilfrid Perrett has traced the Lear story from Geoffrey of Monmouth down through Shakespeare's *King Lear* and has discussed all the various versions and their influence on succeeding versions in his exhaustively documented work, *The Story of King Lear from Geoffrey of Monmouth to Shakespeare*.[36] He points out that, although numerous critics in the nineteenth century assumed that the playwright of *King Leir* had used *Holinshed's Chronicles* as his chief source, the dramatist in fact selected materials from the three most recent metrical versions of the story, all published within just a few years of each other; William Warner's *Albion's England* (1586),[37] the *Mirror for Magistrates* (1587),[38] and Edmund Spenser's *The Faerie Queene* (1590).[39] Perrett is probably correct in his assertion, for if the playwright used Holinshed at all he borrowed only the bare outline of the plot from that source. There is little else in the play that suggests Holinshed as a primary source.

These three versions of the Lear story contain certain materials (incidents, names, relationships) that are peculiar only to them. These materials are not present in earlier versions of the tale; they appear to be the inventions of each of these authors. These same materials appear in the playwright's treatment of the Lear story. On the basis of this evidence, we can assume that the parallels between *King Leir* and these three stories are not just coincidences. It appears that the playwright knew *Albion's England*, the *Mirror*, and *The Faerie Queene*, and incorporated some of their unique features into his own story.

From *Albion's England*, he appears to have borrowed the following: the daughters' attempt on their father's life; the Gallian king's coming to England with his army "of forcie Gawles"; Leir's doting on his three daughters; his attitude after he discovers the elder daughters' hatred of him (he becomes passive and desires his own death); and his increased sorrow when he is reunited with Cordella. In addition, the form of the heroine's name and her husband's title, "the Gallian king," may very well have come from this source.

From the *Mirror for Magistrates* the playwright may have borrowed the idea of jealous elder sisters and their inciting their father's wrath against Cordella at the time of the love-test. Furthermore, help given Leir by his former subjects during the battle may also have been suggested by the *Mirror*.

The playwright appears to have borrowed still other incidents from *The Faerie Queene* (Book II, Canto x): Leir's determination to divide his kingdom equally before putting the love-test to his daughters; the emphasis on the three daughters being equally beautiful; Leir's immediate abdication in favor of his daughters, and the daughters' receipt of their portion by the casting of lots. In other sources, such as Geoffrey, Holinshed, and the *Mirror*, the sons-in-law and the elder daughters take Leir's kingdom from him by force.

Although he may have borrowed these kinds of material from these sources, it seems clear that he did not rely on these earlier versions for phrases and lines of dialogue. Very few passages from the play echo phraseology from the earlier works. The following lines (italics mine) from the earlier stories are the only ones that suggest borrowings:

1. The Eldest did esteeme
   Her life inferior to her love.

   (*Albion's England*, III.xiv.3-4)

   I think my *life inferior to my love.*

   (*King Leir*, iii.42)

2. No greater *ease* of *heart* than *griefes* to tell

   (*Mirror*, stanza 2)

   To utter *grief* doth *ease* a *heart* o'ercharg'd

   (*King Leir*, vii.58)

3. Whose simple answers, wanting colours fair
   To *paint* it *forth,* him to displeasance moov'd.

   (*Fairie Queene*, II.x.stanza 28)

> I cannot *paint* my duty *forth* in words.
>
> (*King Leir*, iii.78)

From this kind of evidence it seems evident that he borrowed certain incidents and forms of names from these earlier stories but did not turn to them for phraseology. The reason for this is that these sources are relatively short stories in a series of other stories. The playwright is writing dialogue, and his story is a long one in comparison to them. There is, therefore, very few lines in these sources that he could draw upon, even if he wished to do so.

From each of these sources, the playwright borrowed various incidents and adopted certain expressions, but at the same time he also created scenes and characters either not present in the other sources or only slightly hinted at. Skalliger and Perillus, although descendents of morality play figures, are not characters suggested in any earlier version of the Lear story; the Messenger, Mumford, the two watchmen and certain minor characters are also additions to the story. Furthermore, there is nothing in any of the earlier versions to suggest the wooing scene between Cordella and Gallia; or the attempted murder of Leir and Perillus by the hired assassin, the Messenger; or the recognition scene between Leir and Cordella. Some of these new personages and the recognition scene, in particular, are later transformed by Shakespeare as he borrows incidents, characters, and phraseology from this old play for use in his own version of the story.

VI. RELATIONSHIP OF *KING LEIR* TO SHAKESPEARE'S *KING LEAR*

On November 26, 1607, the following entry for Shakespeare's *King Lear* appeared in the Stationers' Register;

> Nathaniel Butter   Entred for their copie vnder th [e h] andes
> John Busby   of Sir GEORGE BUCK knight and Th [e] wardens
>   A booke called. Master WILLIAM SHAKESPEARE
>   his *'historye of kinge LEAR'* as yt was
>   played before the kinges maiestie at White-
>   hall uppon Sainct Stephens night [26 December] *at Christmas Last by his maiesties
>   servantes playinge usually at the 'Globe'
>   on the Banksyde.*

When the quarto was published in 1608, it bore the following title:

> M. William Shakespeare: |*HIS*| True Chronicle Historie of the life and | death of King LEAR and his three | Daughters. *With the vnfortunate life of* Edgar, *sonne* | and heire to the Earle of Gloster, and his | sullen and assumed humor of | TOM of Bedlam: *As it was played before the Kings Maiestie at Whithall vpon* S. Stephans *night in Christmas Hollidayes.* | By his Maiesties seruants playing vsually at the Gloabe | on the Bancke-side. | [device 316] LONDON, Printed for *Nathaniel Butter*, and are to be sold at his shop in *Pauls* | Church-yard at the signe of the Pide Bull neere | *St. Austins* Gate. 1608.

This is often referred to as the "Pied Bull" Quarto. [40]

There is little doubt that Shakespeare knew the old play *King Leir*, but whether he used the 1605 edition or an earlier copy of the play as his source is a problem not easily resolved. The date for Shakespeare's composition of *King Lear* is still unsettled. It was written sometime before its first recorded performance before the king on December 26, 1606, at Whitehall, and after the publication of Samuel Harsnet's *Declaration of Egregious Popish Impostures*, recorded in the Stationers' Register on March 16, 1603, from which Shakespeare borrowed or adapted the names of Edgar's devils. The play was therefore written between March 1603 and Christmas 1606. According to Kenneth Muir, the most usual hypothesis for the date of Shakespeare's composition of his play is "that Shakespeare wrote *King Lear* in the winter of 1605-6, and that he used the 1605 edition of *The True Chronicle History of King Leir* which was published after 8 May 1605, when it was entered in the Stationers' Register." [41]

However, several scholars question this hypotheses. First of all, on the title page of the quarto of *King Leir,* the play is called a "True Chronicle History," but the entry of 1605 in the Register describes it as a "Tragecall historie." According to W.W. Greg, this entry suggests that early in 1605 the story of Lear was already known as a tragedy, and "it had never been a tragedy until Shakespeare took it in hand." [42] Hardin Craig supports Greg's argument, using the same evidence to argue for 1605 as the year in which Shakespeare's *King Lear* first appeared on stage.[43] This is not a recent contention. I pointed out earlier that Edmund Malone in 1793 believed that the 1605 publication of *Leir* was made for the purpose of "palming off" the 1594 play as Shakespeare's *King Lear*. Malone thought that the latter was by May 1605 a popular tragedy on the London stage, and that Stafford and Wright took advantage of its popularity to issue a fraudulent edition of the anonymous play in order to deceive the public.

Secondly, Greg also argues that the presence of the term, "True Chronicle History," instead of "tragedy"; the additional information of the "unfortunate life of Edgar" (a subplot not present in the old play); and the prominence of Shakespeare's name on the title page of the Pied Bull quarto of Shakespeare's *King Lear* can perhaps be explained as the desire to Nathaniel Butter to mark his edition as the genuine *Lear* and Wright's edition of the older play as an attempt to capitalize on the prestige of Shakespeare's tragedy.

Thirdly, the publisher indicates on the title page that *King Leir* has been "divers and sundry times lately acted." "Lately" could very well mean anytime within the past two or three years. Furthermore, Greg finds it "very difficult to believe that this respectable but old-fashioned play, dating back in all probability to about 1590 had been 'diuers and sundry times lately acted' in 1605, especially if the play-house manuscript had been for years in the hands of stationers." [44] Kenneth Muir supports Greg's view and adds that if the play had not been recently acted, "it looks very much as though the publishers resurrected the play after a lapse of eleven years, in the hope that it would be mistaken for Shakespeare's new play." [45] It seems clear that if Shakespeare's *King Lear* were on stage in early 1605, the publisher would have a good reason to publish the old *Leir*--to capitalize on the popularity of the newer play. Unfortunately, we have no record showing that Shakespeare's play was being performed at this time.

C.C. Stopes [46] and Geoffrey Bullough [47] offer still another reason for the publication of *King Leir* in 1605. They report the story of Brian Annesley, a servant of Queen Elizabeth. He had three daughters: Grace, Christian, and Cordell. In 1603 the oldest, Grace, tried to have her father judged insane because he was senile and could not manage his affairs. Cordell protested her sister's action. When Annesley died in July 1604 Cordell received most of his estate while her sisters received very little. They contested the will, but the Prerogative Court upheld the will on December 3, 1604. Stopes and Bullough judge that the whole affair, which had received some measure of publicity, may have been in part responsible for the revival of *King Leir* and its publication in 1605. According to Bullough, this domestic dispute may also have affected Shakespeare. "Did Leir's faithful companion become the Earl of Kent because Kent was Annesley's county, or merely because some of the action occurs around Dover?" [48] It is possible that the Annesley case influenced the publication of *King Leir* and also influenced Shakespeare in his writing *King Lear*. Kenneth Muir points out that in none of the fifty or sixty versions of the Lear story before Shakespeare's version does Lear go mad. "Lear's madness may have been suggested to the poet by the madness of Annesley and the loyalty of his Cordella."[49]

If Shakespeare's play were already on stage in early 1605, then Shakespeare surely would not have used the 1605 edition of *King Leir* as his source. W. W. Greg offers a plausible explanation for Shakespeare's having read the old *Leir* before it was published. The play originally belonged to the Queen's Men. Queen Elizabeth's Men was the most famous of all the London acting companies in the 1580's, but by the beginning of the 1590's the men, "whether because they had ceased to be modish, or because their finances had proved unable to stand the strain of the plague years, were now at the end of their London career." [50] A clear indication of this is that on May 8, 1594, Henslowe records in his diary a loan of L15 to his nephew Francis Henslowe "to lay downe for his share to the Queens players when they broke and went into the contrey to playe." [51] Another indication that the company was in financial trouble was the sale of nine of its plays to publishers in 1594 and 1595 (*King Leir* was among those sold); only one of its plays, *The Troublesome Reign of King John,* had been sold and printed before 1594. [52]

Greg's theory is that the moribund Queen's Company indeed sold a manuscript of *King Leir* to White in 1594. Possibly it was a bad text, variously mutilated and debased, so that White did not think that it worth publishing. If this were the case, then the manuscript was certainly not the one printed by Stafford. The manuscript later printed by Stafford may have remained until 1605 in the stock of another acting company, for "it is possible that after the Queen's Men had acted the play at the Rose in April

1594, the prompt book remained as a pledge in Henslowe's hands." From Henslowe, the property would naturally pass to Alleyn who was at the time leading the joint Strange's and Admiral's company. Some of Strange's men were assimilated into the Chamberlain's men and when Strange's company broke up in 1594, and for a short while there was cooperation if not a merger between the Admiral's and Chamberlain's men. [53] "Subsequently, when the Admiral's and Chamberlain's men started on their independent careers, [the prompt book] may have somehow found its way among the effects of the latter." [54] If this series of events did take place, then Shakespeare as a member of the Chamberlain's men would have had access to the play and therefore could have read it and used parts of it as he composed his own play. "After that we have only to assume that he was careless enough to let it get into the nimble hands of Simon Strafford." [55]

Geoffrey Bullough argues, however, that it is easier to believe that Shakespeare had seen *King Leir* on the Jacobean stage and had read it in print than to believe that he used a manuscript which had somehow "come into the possession of the Chamberlain's men." In answer to Greg's notion that he found it difficult to believe that this "old fashioned play" had been acted in 1605, Bullough points out that revivals of older plays were not unknown. "*Mucedorus*, a much looser piece of romantic writing was revived in 1611, with some additions, by Shakespeare's company, before the King." [56] What Bullough does not point out, however, is that *Mucedorus* was one of the most popular plays of the age. It was printed seventeen times from 1598 to 1668.

Kenneth Muir disagrees with the notion that Shakespeare must have read the old play in manuscript:

> But it is really necessary to suppose that Shakespeare had read *King Leir*? If echoes of Coleridge's reading could coalesce years later in *The Ancient Mariner,* echoes which are in some instance closer than anything of *Leir* in *Lear*, why could not Shakespeare have got all he needed from memories of the old play which he might have seen performed in 1594, or before? From such a performance, ten or fifteen years before, he might well have recalled the main outlines of the piece, as well as a few vivid scenes and chance phrases. It might even be suggested that there is a possibility that Shakespeare acted in *King Leir*; and as Perillus is on the

> stage when all save one of the . . . parallel passages are
> spoken, that may have been Shakespeare's role." [57]

There appears to be no solution to the problem of whether Shakespeare read the old play in manuscript or in the 1605 edition, or whether he saw it on stage in 1605 or remembered it from the 1594 performance. However, it seems to be more reasonable to believe that Shakespeare read a manuscript of the play rather than to think he remembered lines from an old play he may have acted in some ten years before. It also seems more reasonable to believe that Shakespeare's *King Lear* was completed and on stage early in 1605. It was its popularity on stage along with the notoriety of the Annesley case that led Stafford to publish the old *King Leir*- - to capitalize on these two events.

Shakespeare's indebtness to the old play has been variously estimated. There seem to be many resemblances between the two plays in both incident and phraseology, but it is difficult to declare with any assuredness where Shakespeare deliberately borrowed from the old play and where the relationship between the two works is only accidental. Nevertheless, Sidney Lee, [58] W.J. Craig, [59] W.W. Greg, [60] and Kenneth Muir [61] have cited many parallels. Some parallels seem to show Shakespeare's conscious borrowing; many seem to be merely coincidental. For instance, the following examples from Greg's list of parallel passages seem to be only accidentally similar. In *King Leir* Leir says to Cordella,

> Why, how now, minion, are you grown so proud?

> (iii.86)

In Shakespeare's play, Lear says to Cordelia,

> How, now, Cordelia? mend your speech a little.

> (I.i.94)

Greg also argues that two other passages echo each other. In *King Leir,* Cornwall says to Gonorill,

> In faith, I fear that all things go not well.

> (x.14)

In *King Lear*, Gloucester speaks to Lear in these words,

I would have all well betwixt you.

(II.iv.120)

In both examples, however, the thoughts expressed and the method of expressing them are so commonplace that to say Shakespeare borrowed them from the old play appears to be a forcing of very slender evidence.

Other parallels, however, seem to be obvious borrowings. The love test episode in both plays is similar, particularly the single line asides in which Cordella comments on her sisters' protestations of love for their father in scene iii of *King Leir*. The kneeling scene from the old play is used by Shakespeare in both the recognition scene and later in the scene in which Lear and Cordelia are led away to prison.

King Leir:

Cord.   But look, dear father; look, behold, and see
        Thy loving daughter speaketh unto thee.
            She kneels,
Leir.   Oh, stand thou up; it is my part to kneel
        And ask forgiveness for my former faults.
            He kneels.
Cord.   Oh, if your wish I should enjoy my breath,
        Dear father rise, or I receive my death.
            He riseth.
Leir.   Then I will rise to satisfy your mind
        But kneel again 'til pardon be resign'd,

(xxiv.203-210)

King Lear:

Cordelia.   O! look upon me, Sir,
            And hold your hand in benediction o'er me
            No, Sir, you must not kneel.

(IV.vii.57-59)

Lear.   When thou dost ask me blessing, I'll kneel down,
            And ask of thee forgiveness.

(V.iii.10-11)

Greg argues that Perillus, the wise counsellor, is the prototype of Kent. Ragan in the old play hires a messenger to murder Leir and Perillus; and in Shakespeare's play, Regan bribes Oswald to murder Gloucester, and Edmund bribes the captain to murder Lear and Cordelia. The thunder that so frightens the Messenger in *Leir* becomes the storm in *King Lear,* and the "'mildness' of Goneril's husband is strikingly anticipated" by the old play. [62]

Greg points out still another instance that suggests Shakespeare's borrowing from the old play. The Fool in *King Lear* says:

> That lord that counsell'd thee
> To give away thy land,
> Come place him here by me,
> Do thou for him stand.

(I.iv. 146-149)

No one counselled the king to do the rash act in Shakespeare's play, but in *King Leir* that advice is given by the bad counsellor, Skalliger,

> I censure thus: your majesty knowing well
> What several suitors your princely daughters have,
> To make them each a jointer more or less,
> As is their worth, to them that love profess.

(i.33-36)

Greg points out that "these are all resemblances of a general character such as might result from recollection of a play seen on the stage several years before. If any more intimate relation is to be found we must look for it in the subtler links of language or of thought." [63] Greg believes that the only case of certain verbal dependence occurs in the third act of *King Lear* when Lear says,

> No, I will be the pattern of all patience;
> I will say nothing.

(III.ii.37-38)

These lines appear to be modelled on Perillus' description of Leir:

> But he, the mirror of mild patience
> Puts up all wrongs and never gives reply.
>
> (viii.12-13)

Kenneth Muir argues that another passage in *King Lear* is an obvious borrowing from the old play. In the old play, Perillus upbraids Gonorill with the words,

> Nay, peace thou monster, shame unto they sex,
> Thou fiend in likeness of a human creature.
>
> (xxix.72-73)

Four lines later, Leir asks Ragan, "Knowest thou these letters?"--letters which she snatches and tears. Similarly in *King Lear*, Albany urges Goneril,

> See thyself, devil!
> Proper deformity shows not in the fiend
> So horrid as in woman.
>
> (IV.ii.59-61)

And in the last scene he says to her,

> Shut your mouth, dame,
> Or with this paper shall I stople it. Hold sir;
> Thou worse than any name, read thine own evil!
> No tearing, lady; I perceive you know it.
> *Gon.* Say, if I do! the laws are mine, not thine;
> Who can arraign me for't?
> *Alb.* Most monstrous! Oh!
> Know'st thou this paper?"
>
> (V.iii.154-161)

"Shame," "fiend," and "know'st thou" are common in both passages; "monster," "sex," and "these letters" are echoed in "monstrous," "woman," and "this paper," and the stage direction in the old play was remembered in Shakespeare's "no tearing." [64]

These scholars point out that numerous other lines from both plays also show some similarity; many of these parallels would perhaps not seem significant were they read as isolated instances, but because there are so many echoes of the old play in *King Lear*, these passages "can hardly be dismissed as fortuitous." [65]

1. The world weariness of Leir in his opening speech,
>   One foot already hangeth in the grave
>   . . . .
>   The world of me, I of the world am weary
>   And I would fain resign these earthly cares.
>
>   (i.22,24-25)

is similarly expressed in Lear's speech:
>   'tis our fast intent
>   To shake all cares and business from our age,
>   Conferring them on younger strengths, while we
>   Unburthened crawl toward death.
>
>   (I.i.38-41)

2. Gonorill speaks to Ragan of Leir,

>   For he, you know, is always in extremes.
>
>   (ii.100)

Goneril echoes the same idea in *Lear*:

>   You see how full of changes his age is
>   . . . .
>   The best and soundest of his time has been
>   but rash.
>
>   (I.i.288,295-296)

3. In the following passage Cordella tells Leir that she is unable to flatter him, that her deeds are far more important than her words, and that she knows what her proper bond is to her father:
>   I cannot paint my duty forth in words;
>   I hope my deeds shall make report for me.
>   But look what love the child doth owe the father,

The same to you, I bear, my gracious lord.

>   (iii.78-81)

In *King Lear*, Cordelia expresses the same ideas:

> Unhappy that I am, I cannot heave
> My heart into my mouth: I love your Majesty
> According to my bond; no more nor less,
> . . . .
> Return those duties back as are right fit.
> . . . .
> If for I want that glib and oily art
> To speak and purpose not, since what I well
>   intend
> I'll do't before I speak.
>
>   (I.i.91-93, 96, 224-6)

4. Perillus speaks of the restraints put on Leir:

> His pension she hath half restrained from him,
> And will ere long the other half, I fear.
>
>   (viii.20-21)

Gonorill tells Skalliger,

> I have restrained half his portion already
> And I will presently restrain the other.
>
>   (ix.34-35)

In *King Lear*, Lear says,

> What, fifty of my followers at a clap?
> Within a fortnight?
>
>   (I.iv.302-303)

And later, Lear complains to Regan of Goneril,

> She hath abated me of half my train.
> . . . .
> To grudge my pleasures, to cut off my train,
> To bandy hasty words, to scant my sizes.
>
>   (II.iv.160,176-177)

5. Gonorill's complaint to Skalliger against her father,

> Could any woman of our dignity
> Endure such quips and peremptory taunts
> As I do daily from my doting father?

(ix.2-4)

is echoed in Goneril's complaint to Oswald in *King Lear*:

> By day and night he wrongs me; every hour
> He flashes into one gross crime or other,
> That sets us all at odds: I'll not endure it:
> His knights grow riotous, and himself upbraids us
> On every trifle.

(I.iii.4-8)

6. A Messenger enters with letters for Leir,

> *Gon.* Let me see them.
> *She opens them.*
> *Mess.* Madam, I hope your grace will stand
> Between me and my neck-verse.
> . . . .
> *Gon.* I tell thee, we make great account of thee.

(xii.49-51,59)

In *Lear*, Oswald brings letters for Edmund,

> *Regan.* . . . I'll love thee much,
> Let me unseal the letter.
> *Osw.* Madam, I had rather--

(IV.v.21--23)

7. The Messenger boasts to Gonorill,

> I will so tongue-whip him that I will
> Leave him as bare of credit. . .

(xii.99-100)

Lear complains to Regan of Goneril,

> She hath abated me of half my train;
> Look'd black upon me; struck me with her tounge,
> Most serpent-like, upon the very heart.
>
> (II.iv.160-162)

8. Perillus questions,

> Oh just Jehovah . . .
> . . . .
> How canst thou suffer such outrageous acts
> To be committed without just revenge?
> Oh viperous generation and accursed,
> To seek his blood, whose blood did make them first.
>
> (xix.204,206-209)

Similarly, Albany declares in *King Lear*,

> If that the heavens do not their visible spirits
> Send quickly down to tame these vild offences,
> It will come,
> Humanity must perforce prey on itself,
> Like monsters of the deep.
>
> (IV.ii.46-50)

9. Gallia speaks to Cordella of Leir,

> Forebear awhile until his strength return
> Lest, being overjoyed with seeing thee,
> His poor weak senses should forsake their office.
> And so cause of joy be turn'd to sorrow.
>
> (xxiv.103-106)

The Doctor says to Cordelia of Lear,

> Be comforted, good Madam; the great rage,
> You see, is killed in him: and yet it is danger
> To make him even o'er the time he has lost,

> Desire him to go in; trouble him no more
> Till further settling.
>
> (IV.iii.78-82)

Similarly, Edgar says of Gloucester,

> but his flaw'd heart,
> Alack, too weak the conflict to support!
> 'Twixt two extremes of passion, joy and grief,
> Burst smilingly.
>
> (V.iii.196-199)

10. Cambria declares that,

> The heavens are just and hate impiety.
>
> (xxii.30)

and Edgar tells his brother in *Lear* that,

> The gods are just, and of our pleasant vices
> Make instruments to plague us.
>
> (V.iii.170-171)

11. Leir's words, although not spoken directly to Ragan in *King Leir*,

> Ah, cruel Ragan, did I give thee all,

are echoed in Lear's words to Regan,

> I gave you all.
>
> (II.iv.252)

Greg lists numerous other passages in *King Lear* that seem to echo ideas or phraseology from the old play, but they show less similarity than the ones cited above. Nevertheless, all the passages considered together indicate that Shakespeare knew *King Leir* in one form of the other. "Ideas, phrases, cadences from the old play still floated in his memory . . . and now and again one or another helped to fashion the words that flowed from his pen." [66]

VII. A CRITICAL READING

The author of *King Leir* calls his play a history, and he presents figures which were accepted as historical in Elizabethan times. But he treats these figures as ordinary human beings who show little interest in the affairs of state except in the very first and the very last scenes. The play, though called a chronicle history when it was first entered in the Stationers' Register is in fact a romance, belonging to that class of plays thath uses chronicle material together with romantic or comic ingredients, [67] sharing most of the characteristics associated with Robert Greene's *The Scottish History of James the Fourth* and *Friar Bacon and Friar Bungay, Mucedorus, A Knack to Know a Knave*, and Shakespeare's *Cymbeline*.

In his introduction to *Pericles, Prince of Tyre* James G. McManaway outlines the characteristics of the romance: "Characters are two-dimensional and static: the good are very good and the evil have no redeeming feature." There are exotic settings, shipwrecks, miraculous restoration from apparent death, rescue from the sea, and, above all, "recognition and reconciliations and the healing of breaches or the righting of ancient injuries." The themes of the romance are patience, constancy, and forgiveness, and the dramatic interest is focused upon recognition scenes. [68] Karl Holzknecht lists other characteristics: love at first sight, frequent disguises, the sylvan poetic scenes, idyllic love, misunderstandings, witticisms, clownage, the timely deliverance of the hero from danger, and the happy ending. [69]

Many of these characteristics are found in *King Leir*. Cordella and the king of Gallia fall in love and marry on the day of their first meeting. Gallia in disguise as a palmer courts Cordella, and later both of them, disguised as peasants, chance to meet the destitute Leir and Perillus dressed in seamen's gowns and caps. Leir's misinterpreting his older daughters' flattery and Cordella's wise saying lead to Cordella's exile, and later the filial ingratitude of the two villainous sisters leads to Leir's pathetic suffering and threatened death. But banishment, exile, and separation are followed by reunion, restoration, and the avenging of all wrongs. Interspersed throughout the play are the witticisms of Mumford and the diabolical Messenger along with the clownage of the two watchmen. From this summary of characteristics, it is apparent that the playwright, as he wrote his play, tapped most of the elements associated with a romance.

Records of the Revels Office provide ample evidence of the vogue at Court of romances during the period 1570-1595. The titles of sixty-three plays, most of them lost, are listed as having been presented at court during those years. Of these, at least twenty-three, according to Alfred Harbage, are classified as romantic plays on the basis of their titles. [70] Among some of those listed are *The Painter's Daughter* (1576); *The Irish Knight* (1577); *The Blacksmith's Daughter* (1578); Robert Greene's *Alphonsus, King of Aragon* (1587); John Lyly's *Campaspe* (1584) and *Galatea* (1588). Simultaneously, the chronicle play was developing in the public playhouses during this period. The following plays are representative: *I and II The Troublesome Reign of King John* (1588); Munday's *John a Kent and John a Cumber* (1589); Greene's *The Scottish History of James IV* (1590); Peele's *Edward I* (1591); Shakespeare's *II and III Henry VI* (1591); and Marlowe's *Edward II* (1592). The nationalistic spirit of Elizabethan England suggested to playwrights a new field of subject matter, the glories and vicissitudes of England's past. Between the days of the Spanish Armada and the close of Elizabeth's reign, approximately one play in every five had at least a background of English history. The mixing of these two genres, the romance and the chronicle history, provided playwrights with further possibilities for dramatic material.

An interesting feature often found in some of these chronicle-romances is the "disguised ruler," a feature used in *King Leir*. Rulers in disguise were popular figures on the stage in the 1590's, as in *Fair Em* (1590), *George a Greene* (1590), *Edward I* (1591), *A Knack to Know a Knave* (1592), Shakespeare's *Henry V* (1599), *The First Part of King Edward IV* (1599), and *Part I of Sir John Oldcastle* (1599). The figures of kings in disguise were used for romance, light comedy, for popular exposures of low life, and, as J.W. Lever points out, "for a more critical, self-wounding expression of social malaise"[71] in the early years of the new century. Anne Barton discusses this particular literary device, its background and its significance, in an article "The King Disguised: Shakespeare's *Henry V* and the Comical History." [72]

According to her, the king's disguise is seen in all these early plays as a romantic gesture. The kings mask themselves in search for the unusual, the marvellous, and the strange. The people they meet come from legend and ballad, characters nurtured in the popular imagination of the time: Robin Hood, Maid Marian, thieves, beggars, the beggarmaid who is destined to become queen, the honest miller, among others. In the meeting between disguised king and commoner, both discover that they share a "unanimity of opinion and mutual respect." Disguise is an essential prerequisite for the ease and success of the meeting between private man and king, and disguise is the means by which the ruler can discover the true spirit of the men and women he meets. Their meeting and the subsequent righting of all wrongs are the "wish-dream of a peasantry harried and perplexed by a new class of officials, an impersonal bureaucracy against which the ordinary man seemed to have no redress." [73] This fiction represented how easily and readily justice might be attained if only the lowly subject could speak one-to-one with his sovereign. "In its most serious form it confirmed the central humanist concept of royal authority, according to which the true ruler set an example of wisdom, temperance, and magnanimity." [74] This attractive fantasy is far removed from anything which the hard-headed citizens of Elizabethan London actually believed; nevertheless, it was a popular tradition, one which most Elizabethan dramatists used from time to time.

    The disguised ruler convention appears in *King Leir* with the disguised Gallian king meeting Cordella after her expulsion from her father's court. The young king, falling in love with her at first sight, claims he has been sent by his sovereign to make her the Gallian queen. She, thinking he is a poor pilgrim, falls in love with him and rejects the offer to become the Gallian queen. Instead, she asks him to woo her for himself; when the young king discovers she loves the man and not the monarch, he reveals his identity; they are married and then return to France. Later in the play, disguise is used again by the couple as they mingle with their subjects and then discover the destitute Leir and Perillus on the seacoast of their country. The playwright's use of the "king disguised convention and his ample employment of the characteristics of the romance genre, all cast in the framework of the chronicle play shows that *King Leir* was very much a part of what was popular stage fare in the early 1590's.

Over the years, critics have had faint praise for *King Leir*, giving more attention to it as one of Shakespeare's primary sources for his play than for any artistic value the old play may have in itself. Lewis Theobald found nothing good to say about it, calling it a "most execrable dramatic performance."[75] Edward Capell called it a "silly old play" which "creeps in one dull tenor." [76] He did, however, comment favorably on the kneelng scene as "a circumstance of some beauty which Shakespeare borrowed" and of the watchmen scene as containing "some low humor passable enough." [77] John P. Collier said of the play that there was "nothing more tame and mechanical than the whole of the dialogue of the Chronicle History which Malone with great injustice conjectures to have been written by Thomas Kyd." [78] Charles Knight, while admitting its inferiority as "compared with the wonderful production of Shakspere," is "by no means certain that it is not as good as half the pieces which occupied the stage, and not unsuccessfully, at the very time that Shakespeare had produced some of his most glorious works." [79] Alolphus William Ward in his *History of English Dramatic Literature* gave the play little praise: "In general the old play is in diction of the poorest and baldest character, but with all its defects the play seems only to await the touch of a powerful hand to be converted into a tragedy of supreme effectiveness, and while Shakspere's genius nowhere exerted itself with more transcendent force and marvellous versatility, it nowhere found more promising materials ready to its command." [80] John Addington Symonds, however, claims that *King Leir* takes a "higher rank than *Locrine*. The unknown writer of the piece deals in the sober spirit of an honest craftsman with the old English legend. The style is plain and sturdy, free from the intolerable pedantries and pettinesses of Greene's mythologizing school." [81] Symonds also praises the "power in the characterizations of the three sisters and the pathos in the situation of Leir and Perillus." [82] On the other hand, Sidney Lee finds little to redeem the play: "Apart from its Shakespearian association, the drama only deserves attention as a specimen of the humble average fare which commended itself to the Elizabethan play-goer." [83] Felix Schelling speaks of the play's "genuine intrinsic worth." To him the old play retains "a merit of its own, especially in the simple candor and beauty of the character of Cordella." He was deeply touched by the wooing scene which "is as naive as it is poetical." [84] H.H. Furness calls it "a good specimen of the third class of comedies" [85] of that period, while Hardin Craig characterizes it as "a rather bright and cheerful play" which furnished events for Shakespeare's *King Lear*, but "did not furnish tone, atmosphere, the deeper significance of the play [*Lear*] and the tragic concept." [86] Symonds praises the playwright's "plain and sturdy" style; it is true that in comparison with some of the drama of the 1590's it is remarkably free from bombast and from classical conceits for a play of this period. Nevertheless this plain and sturdy style is far too often wooden and ponderous. The metrical monotony of his verse is mechanical and hardly changes pace whether a character is expressing anger, love, remorse, or joy. Ragan's anxiety in the following lines is conveyed only by the words she speaks. The plodding rhythm and the erratic use of rhyme prevent the speech from catching fire:

> I feel a hell of conscience in my breast,
> Tormenting me with horror for my fact,
> And makes me in an agony of doubt,
> For fear the world should find my dealing out.
> The slave whom I appointed for the act,
> I ne'er set eye upon the peasant since.
> Oh, could I get him for to make him sure,
> My doubts would cease and I should rest secure.
>
> (xxiv.1-8)

Cordella expresses her love for the disguised king of Gallia in these lines:

> I'll hold thy palmer's staff within my hand
> And think it is the scepter of a queen.
> Sometime I'll set thy bonnet on my head
> And think I wear a rich imperial crown.
> Sometime I'll help thee in thy holy prayers
> And think I am with thee in Paradise.
> Thus I'll mock Fortune as she mocketh me,
> And never will my lovely choice repent;
> For having thee, I shall have all content.
>
> (vii.115-124)

There is a certain sweetness in the lines spoken, but they lack the fervor or intensity one might expect from a young lady declaring her love for someone.

Although the playwright wrote most of the play in blank verse, he also used much rhyme and some prose. But even though he uses rhyme throughout the play, he is not consistent in its use. He will move from blank verse to rhyme and back again without any apparent reason. For example, one of Leir's speeches in the opening scene mixes the two:

> Herein, my lords, your wishes sort with mine,
> And mine, I hope, do sort with heavenly powers;
> For at this instant two near neighboring kings,
> Of Cornwall and of Cambria, motion love
> To my two daughters, Gonorill and Ragan.
> My youngest daughter, fair Cordella, vows
> No liking to a monarch, unless love allows.
> She is solicited by divers peers,
> But none of them her partial fancy hears.
> Yet, if my policy may her beguile,
> I'll match her to some king within this isle
> And so establish such a perfect peace
> As fortune's force shall ne'er prevail to cease.
>
> (i.54-66)

In this speech the first five lines are blank verse while the following eight lines are rhymed.

In a monologue of Ragan (xxii.12-29), there are eight successive lines rhymed alternately; almost all the other lines are rhymed couplets. In other monologues (Perillus' in viii.1-29 and Cordella's in xiii.1-32) no such pattern occurs; rhyme and blank verse are mixed indiscriminately. In the last speech of the play, the final twenty lines are rhymed successively.

Every speech in the first scene closes with a couplet. This characteristic occurs quite often throughout the play (particularly in the monologues), but not with the consistency it is used in the first scene. When the rhymed couplet does occur in the other scenes, it usually comes only at the end of longer speeches. But even this usage is erratic; a few of the longer speeches do not end in couplets, while some shorter speeches (four of five lines long) do. There is no logical pattern in the playwright's usage.

He employs several kinds of rhyme schemes. He uses double rhyme occasionally:

> Do now reject, condemn, despise, *abhor me*,
> What reason moveth thee to sorrow *for me*?
>
> (x.87-88)
>
> I will to church and pray unto my *Savior*
> That, ere I die, I may obtain his *favor*.
>
> (xiii.31-32)
>
> Oh her, dear heart, whom I for no *occasion*
> Turn'd out of all through flatterers' *persuasion*;
>
> (xxiv.64-65)

There are at least two instances of identical rhyme:

> Am I awake, or is it but *a dream*?
> Fear nothing, man, thou art but in *a dream*.
>
> (xix.172-173)
>
> For promise is debt, and by this hand, you promis'd *it me*.
> Therefore, you owe it me, and you shall pay *it me*.
>
> (xxi.44-45)

And at least one internal rhyme:

> I like the *wooing* that's not long *a-doing*.
>
> (vii.155)

There are numerous examples of alliteration. Among them are the following:

> The *w*orld of me, I of the *w*orld am *w*eary.
>
> (i.24)
>
> No *l*iking to a monarch, un*l*ess love a*ll*ows.
>
> (i.60)
>
> He *m*eans to *m*atch *m*e with the Cornwall *k*ing.
>
> (ii.83)

>The *l*ady's *l*ove I *l*ong ago possess'd
>
>(v.39)

>But his old *d*oting *d*oltish withered wit.
>
>(ix.11)

>You may go pack, and *s*eek *s*ome other place,
>To *s*ow the *s*eed of di*s*cord and di*s*grace.
>
>(x.35-36)

The playwright's wide use of various rhyming patterns indicates that he may have been playing with as many kinds of rhyme schemes as possible as he wrote the play. He shows the same inconsistent use of these patterns as he does with mixing rhyme with blank verse; there seems to be no particular reason for his employing double rhyme in one speech and identical rhyme in another. This erratic usage indicates perhaps that he was not concerned with achieving any particular effects by his varying patterns, but that he was merely experimenting with these various poetic devices.

The playwright follows the fairly common practice of having his comic figures and members of the lower class speak in prose; Mumford, the companion of the king of Gallia, and the Messenger alternate between prose and occasionally rather halting verse. Feminine endings are very common in their speeches. The mariners and watchmen use prose throughout. All the other characters, the members of nobility, speak in blank verse, except Gonorill who upon one occasion drops into conversational prose (xii.86-94) as does Cambria in his final speech (xxix.136-38). All in all, the playwright's blank verse, his metrics, and his attempts at various rhyme patterns are for the most part mechanical and uninspired. But although these are defects in the play, the drama still has other more positive qualities.

Irving Ribner calls it "a sentimental fairy story with no historical pretensions," [87] but in discussing its theme, Geoffrey Bullough argues that this "by no means contemptible play" is more than "a sentimental fairy story." Bullough says that "it is a tale in which parental unkindness and filial ingratitude, sins against natural and divine law, are contrasted with loyalty, truth and piety." [88] And

Madeleine Doran speaks of the highly ethical nature of the play: it demonstrates "the danger of heeding flattery rather than truthful, if plain, speaking," and "contrasts filial ingratitude with true filial piety." [89]

Bullough also points out that the play has strong religious overtones. For example, Leir expresses pious wishes for his dead wife and then wishes to resign his earthly cares, "And think upon the welfare of my soule" (i.26). Cordella is obedient to God's will when she is banished by Leir; she also desires to aid her lover in his holy prayers; and she feels guilty for not going to "the Temple of my God" to give thanks for all his mercies. Furthermore, when she meets her father again, she is filled with love and Christian forgiveness.

The union of divine and natural law is stressed throughout the play. Emphasis is given to the exercise of "kindness," human nature at its best, working by grace through Cordella and Perillus. Perillus' words, "No worldy gifts but grace from God on high, / Doth nourish virtue and true charity." (xix.325-26), underscore the "kindness" theme in the play, and the evil sisters exemplify the "unkindness" in their hatred and cruelty. In scene xix the thunder and lightning is clearly used as a sign of divine Providence when the Messenger attempts the murder of Leir and Perillus. However, the Messenger is not moved by this sign alone; he is moved by the pleas of the old men, thereby showing that he has "some spark of grace." The rest of the play, with the kindness of the mariners, Cordella's loving forgiveness, the reconciliation of Leir and Cordella, and the military victory, all, according to Bullough, justify the ways of God to men. [90]

King Leir is a tightly constructed play with the several strands of the plot woven together fairly well. Only one scene can be eliminated without violating the play's unity. That is scene v depicting the journey of Cornwall and Cambria to Leir's court at Troynovant. The two kings are introduced in this scene, but we get no new information from them nor does the action of the play move forward. And what we learn about them could have been revealed in the next scene when they arrive at Leir's court.

In his handling of the separate strands of the plot, the playwright moves back and forth from one to another with relative ease, although he does so quite mechanically. He springs no surprises on his audience but prepares the audience for each new turn in the action. Furthermore, he leaves no loose ends nor incomplete lines of action. To illustrate these two points we have only to look at a minor episode in the plot: an ambassador is to go to Leir with letters of reconciliation from Cordella. In scene xii Cordella expresses to her husband her keen desire for reconciliation with her father; in xvi we learn that an ambassador is to be sent by Gallia to Leir; the ambassador arrives in Cornwall in scene xviii just after Leir's departure; in scene xx the ambassador is to leave for Cambria in search of Leir; and in scene xxii he arrives there. But after Ragan interviews him and then strikes him for his insubordination, the ambassador exits for the last time in the play, but not before pronouncing that a means will be found to "remedy this wrong." From this summary we can see that the playwright paid careful attention to the details of the plot. Characters do not enter and then disappear without some reason. All strands of the plot are neatly tied by the end of the play.

But despite its unity and clarity in movement, the play is still very crudely constructed. For example, the contrivance of having the four kings--Leir, Gallia, Cornwall, and Cambria--wandering through the countryside, "slenderly accompanied," adds to the woodenness of the plot, rather than enriching the texture of the drama with what could potentially be a highly effective use of parallel action. Another example is that on five different occasions (scenes viii, xi, xiii, xx, and xxv), a single character comes on stage, gives information to the audience, then leaves the stage without having significantly assisted the progress of the action. To illustrate, Perillus in scene viii informs us of Leir's patient suffering at the hands of Gonorill and how he (Perillus) will assist Leir in what ways he can. In scene xi Ragan gloats over her new power as queen and informs the audience of her desired plans for her father, "if he were with me"; and in scene xx the ambassador from Gallia informs the audience of his ill treatment by Gonorill and of his intention to go to Cambria to find Leir. In all these scenes the speakers reveal action that has happened, then comment on that action, and finally tell the audience of their intended action.

This expository technique, if not handled well, can be wooden. Its presence in this play only underscores the playwright's lack of skill in being able to develop complications and to create highly dramatic moments. He often has his characters relate events, telling the audience what has happened or what will happen, rather than revealing situation and character through dramatic conflict. Consequently, the dramatist often undercuts the dramatic impact by so much of this telling. For example, Perillus' speech in scene viii, although informative, diminishes the impact of the confrontation between Leir and Gonorill in scene x; we know how Gonorill will behave and how Leir will react before they meet in scene x:

> But he [Leir], the mirror of mild patience,
> Puts up all wrongs and never gives reply.
> Yet shames she [Gonrill] not in most approbrious sort
> To call him fool and dotard to his face.
>
> (viii.12-15)

Scene x, therefore, is little more than a portrayal of Perillus' words in scene viii. The fault is not that the action in scene x is anticipated in scene vii--a standard dramatic trick--but that scene x does not go beyond the anticipation, and so seems redundant.

In the hands of a more skillful playwright, this expository technique can be very effective. Shakespeare in his *Richard III* used the technique to good advantage. Richard steps forward several times to review past actions and reveal his plans for various other people in the play. Even though we know what Richard is like and what he will do, we still watch with fascination as the events unfold, delighting in *how* it is all done, how Richard manipulates and controls the development and the unfolding of events. Rather than lessening the dramatic effect, Richard's asides enhance it. But the playwright of *Leir* clearly lacks that skill. He is at most an adequate expositor of action.

Nor is he very skillful in creating a consistent and sustained dramatic effect. The kneeling scene (scene xxiv) illustrates this. The scene is touching in its conception (Shakespeare obviously recognized that and borrowed it), but before the scene ends it has become ludicrous. Leir and Cordella kneel and rise, confess, and forgive far too many times. Then the King of Gallia kneels, vowing to root out "this viperous sect" and repossess Leir of his crown. And finally Mumford, the wisecracking companion of

Gallia, kneels too, but his vow is that if he returns from England "without my wench, / Let me be gelded for my recompense" (xxiv.258-9). It is apparent from this scene that the playwright had some sense of what could be dramatically effective, but it is also clear that, despite his sensitivity, he lacked the skill to develop that effect properly. What could have been a very moving episode becomes farcical in this playwright's hands.

He spoils another dramatic effect in scene x. In this scene, Leir begins lamenting to Perillus his pitiful state and the injustices done him by Gonorill:

> Oh, how thy words add sorrow to my soul
> To think of my unkindness to Cordella,
> Whom causeless I did dispossess of all
> Upon th'unkind suggestions of her sisters;
> And for her sake I think this heavy doom
> Is fall'n on me, and not without desert.

(x.94-9)

Leir's realization of his predicament, accompanied by this woeful speech, comes too early in the play, long before he has any dealings with his second daughter, Ragan. It is, therefore, not dramatically effective. The playwright has failed to portray a gradual realization in Leir of the consequences of his rash act. Furthermore, Leir's insight comes effortlessly. There is no struggle in him to comprehend what is happening to him. He quickly comes to the conclusion that he has brought all this upon himself and that he deserves it. His conclusion, therefore, lacks much dramatic interest.

For the most part, the playwright's characterizations are as unskilled and mechanical as his plot, although he does occasionally breathe brief vitality into some of his creations. The character of Cordella, for example, is of more than fleeting interest. Plain spoken, sincere, and childlike in her simplicity, she has won the approval of many critics who have had only scant praise for the play otherwise. Schelling praises Cordella's "simple candor and beauty," [91] and H. H. Furness believes that "justice has never been done . . . to the unaffected loveliness of Cordella's character in this old play. She is more lovely and loveable than Cordelia in the first act of *Lear*." [92] Furness points out, in particular, the "womanly tenderness which marks Cordella's conduct towards her broken and repentant old father in the later scenes." [93] Her candor and directness with her sisters, her father, and later with Gallia (when, believing him to be a palmer, she says she would marry the palmer himself rather than the king), her childlike manner, her sincere piety, and her lack of guile make her memorable. "An honest and plain dealing wench," as Mumford describes her, she is by far the most successfully conceived character in the play. Nevertheless, the fullness of characterization that marks the finest Elizabethan drama was simply beyond the ability of this playwright.

The playwright's conception of Leir is clear and consistent after scene iii, but in the opening scenes the playwright shows an inconsistency in his portrayal of the king. In scene i Skalliger suggests to Leir that the daughter who professes the greatest love for him should be the one who gets the greatest share from him, but Leir rejects that suggestion outright: "No more, nor less, but even all alike." Then almost immediately Leir decides to carry out the love test, speaking as if it were his own idea, one which had just occurred to him:

>   I am resolv'd, and even now my mind
>   Doth meditate a sudden strategem
>   To try which of my daughters loves me best.

(i.75-8)

Despite this reversal, Leir's motive is clear. His wife is dead; he wants to resign the crown and live a contemplative life; and his two elder daughters have suitors they are prepared to marry. Cordella, however, has no one, and Leir is concerned that she be cared for. But Cordella will only marry for love. So Leir's strategem of employing the love test is to trick Cordella into marriage with the king of Brittany. His plan is that when Cordella tells him she loves him the best, he will make one request of her, "Accept a husband whom myself will woo." She will not be able to refuse him, and he will have his way. From these opening lines, his motive for arranging his love-test are rational and good-hearted. However, his rejection of Cordella in scene iii is irrational and cold. It is totally unexpected. Nothing in Leir's demeanor up to this point had even hinted that his rejection of Cordella was a possibility. This inconsistency in his character is, therefore, troublesome.

Leir is a shallow creation, lacking any kind of complexity of personality. He is portrayed as a virtuous and an affectionate old man, given to self pity, and he suffers for a short time because of a foolish mistake. His chief desire is for a quiet life of preparation for heaven and then a peaceful death. There is none of the rage in him one would expect from an old king who has had to undergo the humiliation and the torment he experiences later. He becomes angry only once with Cordella very early in the play (scene iii), and that happens because she does not give the response he expects in the love-test. After this one outburst Leir is passive as he undergoes the suffering and the degradation inflicted by his two older daughters' rejection of him, accepting his daughters' displeasure without question and often excusing their actions to others. He is weak, pitiable, and foolish. Once he is reconciled with Cordella, he is restored to his former happiness, having gained, however, little insight or self knowledge. The playwright's portrayal of Leir does not inspire our concern or enthusiasm.

Gonorill and Ragan, the evil sisters, are at heart very much alike, but the playwright has created in these two women fairly distinct personalities. Both women are rude and vicious, but of the two the hypocritical and sly Ragan is more subtle and quiet than her forthright sister. For the most part Ragan reveals what she is only in her monologues. In contrast, Gonorill is distinctly outspoken and has a curious habit of deliberately misunderstanding a speaker's words whenever it suits her purpose to do so. There are several instances when she does this. One such occasion is Leir's excusing her bad temper by attributing it to her possible pregnancy (scene x). Gonorill deliberately misconstrues her father's words to make it appear he had impugned her honor to have accused her of having been unchaste before her marriage. Later, in scene xviii, Gonorill again displays her propensity to twist meaning in her long dialogue with the ambassador from France. This scene is of particular interest because the playwright has created a fairly effective battle of wits between these two. The ambassador in his few lines displays a personality capable of holding its own with the devious Gonorill without allowing her to intimidate him or distort his meaning. He will not permit her to misunderstand him, nor will he allow Gonorill to answer him without clarifying her meaning.

Of Cambria, Cornwall, and Gallia, not so much can be said. They are kind men who are largely influenced by their respective wives. Sidney Lee observes, however, that Cambria's and Cornwall's growing disillusionment with their wives is original with this playwright, not being present in earlier versions of the Lear story.[94] Aside from that observation, these men lack much dramatic interest.

Each of the four comic characters has distinct personalities. Mumford wisecracks constantly; he works very hard to make funny speeches. The First and Second Watchmen are close kin to Shakespeare's Dogberry and his Watch in *Much Ado About Nothing*. Like Shakespeare's two characters, these men are given to malapropisms and other absurdities of speech and logic. Even though the playwright has given these two only thirty-two lines, he has with moderate success sketched two fairly clever comic figures.

Of the four comic figures, the Messenger (the murderer) is the most interesting. Mean, selfish, and mercenary, he is still not altogether a stock villain. He has a grim humor, and he overflows with wit; he shows these qualities in practically every speech, whether he is plotting with Gonorill or threatening to murder Leir and Perillus. In the murder scene his dark humor has full play; the dialogue would otherwise have been very long and very tedious without his cleverness. Not only does he have humor and wit, he also has a "spark of grace." When it thunders twice in the murder scene (a sign of divine Providence), the messenger is shaken. This is not the only reason he does not murder Leir and Perillus; he is influenced by their pleas. He then lets fall the daggers and leaves the men behind. In sharp contrast to the unrepentant sisters, the grim yet witty Messenger shows he has a remnant of goodness in him.

Skalliger, the evil counsellor, and Perillus, the good counsellor, are descendants of morality play figures. Skalliger is particularly interesting because it is his bad advice that provides the impetus for the conflict between Leir and his daughters. When Leir prepares to divest himself of his kingdom, Skalliger suggests that Leir test his daughters' love for him, adding that more wealth should be given to the daughter who professes the greatest love. Leir accepts Skalliger's test proposal against the good Perillus' wise warnings, but Leir rejects the suggestion to make each daughter "a jointure more or less, / As is their worth, to them that love profess." Leir wants to use this scheme to trick Cordella into marrying the prince of Leir's choice. Skalliger goes to Gonorill and Ragan to warn them of the forthcoming test, and despite what Leir has said, tells them that the one who answers best "shall have most unto their marriages." In a later scene Skalliger displays a strong influence on Gonorill. When she prepares to cut off half of Leir's allowance, Skalliger encourages her to cut off all of Leir's allowance, thereby leaving him destitute. As Leir had done earlier, Gonorill follows Skalliger's advice. When Gonorill exits, however, Skalliger reveals his contempt for the woman he has helped, calling her "a viperous woman, shame to all thy sex." In this same speech he also justifies his evil behavior: "he that cannot flatter cannot live." Both times that he gives advice, it is accepted, and in both instances, it propels the characters into further conflicts.

In contrast to Leir, who is foolish and morally blind, the practical Perillus, the good counsellor, is a wise man. He warns Leir against the love test, against forcing "love, where fancy cannot dwell." But once Leir blunders and begins to experience the consequences of that blunder, Perillus remains fiercely loyal to him, not dwelling on past mistakes or insults. Throughout the play, in the face of Leir's despair and pessimism, Perillus is hopeful and optimistic. When Gonorill rejects Leir, Perillus reminds him that he has "two daughters left to whom I know / You shall be welcome, if you please to go" (x.92-3). Later, after the Messenger has spared their lives, Perillus bolsters Leir's sagging hopes, prodding him to overcome his despair and seek out Cordella, reminding him that "She said her love unto you was as much / As ought a child to bear unto her father" (xix.329-30). In stark contrast to Leir's passivity and acceptance of his situation, Perillus is incensed at the injustice done Leir. When they discover that Gonorill and Ragan have plotted Leir's death, Leir gives up and is willing to "submit us to the will of God," but Perillus rages at God for allowing these unjust acts:

> Oh just Jehovah, whose almighty power
> Doth govern all things in this spacious world,
> How canst thou suffer such outrageous acts
> To be committed without just revenge?

(xix.204-207)

Nevertheless, Perillus, rather than remaining alive after Leir's death, "most willingly will have a share in death" (xix.243) with Leir.

There is no doubt that *King Leir* is a flawed work. The playwright is a better expositor of action than he is a creator of consistent and sustained dramatic effects. Furthermore, although his characters show some traces of humanity from time to time, they for the most part demonstrate most clearly that this dramatist lacked the "power of vital characterization." [95] Nevertheless, the play is not completely without merit. Wolfgang Clemen notes that "the plot is very skillfully put together, and is comprehensive and logical in its development." [96] And Robert A. Law observes that the careful, even tedious exposition occurring in many scenes demonstrates that the characters' motivations in *King Leir* are quite often much "clearer than Shakespeare's version." [97]

VIII. MODERN EDITIONS

King Leir was not reprinted until late in the eighteenth century when George Steevens included it in a two-volume edition [98] containing works Shakespeare used as sources for some of his plays. *King Leir* appeared in the second volume. His text is an old-spelling edition and follows the original text very closely. There are few errors; he provides neither notes nor commentary on the play. Nearly a hundred years later *King Leir* was printed again, this time in W. C. Hazlitt's edition of J. P. Collier's *Shakespeare's Library*. [99] This text is also an old-spelling edition and is without notes or commentary. The text has many typographical errors. Neither Steevens nor Hazlitt designate acts or scenes in their editions. In 1907 W. W. Greg edited the play for the Malone Society in a very accurate type facsimile. [100] The lines are numbered consecutively; scene divisions, a list of *dramatis personae*, and a list of irregular and doubtful readings are provided for the first time. Greg used the two copies in the British Museum in the preparation of this text.

In 1909 Sidney Lee edited the play for The Shakespeare Library. [101] Lee provides a long introduction in which he explores such matters as the date of the play, its general characteristics, authorship, background and sources, and the play's influence on Shakespeare's play. He also provides a list of *dramatis personae*, and a glossary and scholarly notes, quoting from contemporary works to illustrate interesting or puzzling parts of the text. Apparently Lee saw too that a part of his task was to smooth out and correct some archaisms and what appeared to be ungrammatical constructions. His changes are noted in this present edition. Lee is the first editor to divide the play into five acts and to provide settings for each scene.

Rudolf Fischer in 1914 reprinted the play in English with a German translation on the facing page.[102] Apparently Fischer used Hazlitt's text for his copy, for he duplicates some of the spelling errors of that edition, but he follows Lee's example by providing settings and act and scene divisions. His act and scene divisions, however, are not the same as Lee's. Fischer also supplied numerous additional stage directions, some of which are very helpful in clarifying some of the play's action.

In 1973 Geoffrey Bullough reprinted the play, an old-spelling edition, in *Narrative and Dramatic Sources of Shakespeare*.[103] The text has no errors. Bullough follows the example of the Malone Society in numbering the lines consecutively throughout the play and in supplying scene numbers only. In his introduction Bullough does an analysis of the play, discussing its themes and its relationship to the traditional Lear story. He also discusses the play's influence on Shakespeare's *Lear*, and provides a few notes on certain passages.

IX. EDITORIAL PROCEDURES

This edition is a modernized critical edition based on the 1605 quarto. There are two kinds of notes: variant substantive readings and explanatory notes that gloss obsolete words and phrases. Emendations of substantives are noted in the textual footnotes. The explanatory notes are located at the bottom of the text to which they refer. Although catchwords and running titles are not reproduced, the signature of each leaf is indicated next to the first line of that leaf.

The form of textual notes is as follows: the line number, the present reading followed by a square bracket, the source of that reading, and other readings and their sources. The notes may refer to emendations as does this example from scene xxii:

15. loss] Lee, Bullough; less Q. Steevens, Hazlitt, Fischer. This may be read, "*loss* is a correction of what appears to have been a printer's error in Q. Lee in his edition of the play was the first editor to make the correction; Bullough agrees with Lee. *Less* is the original spelling in Q, and the editors Steevens, Hazlitt, and Fischer follow Q's spelling in their editions."

All four copies of the 1605 quarto have been collated along with all the editions of the eighteenth, nineteenth, and twentieth centuries. Any errors the compositors may have made in the composition of the text, such as turned letters, wrong font, or any other literal errors, are not recorded unless another word is created by the error.

Words are generally glossed only once, on their first appearance, and glosses not in quotation marks are from the *OED*. Works referred to frequently are given in the list of abbreviations that precedes the text of the play. Those works cited more than once that are not in the list are given full bibliographical form only on their first appearance.

In the treatment of the text itself, contracted forms of characters' names are expanded in speech prefixes. Line numbers have been added. Additions to the stage directions of the basic copy are enclosed in brackets.

The scene divisions, established by the Malone Society in its edition, are used in this text, except for scenes marked 30, 31, and 32 in the Malone Society Reprint. These three scene divisions have been eliminated in the present edition, since the action beginning with scene 29 is continuous to the end of the play. According to the custom of the Elizabethan public stage, a new scene begins whenever the stage is clear and the action is not continuous. The action beginning with scene 29 is a battle; and even though one set of characters replaces another several times, the locale does not change and the action is continuous. For these reasons, it is best to follow the Elizabethan custom of not dividing up the scene.

Greg points out that "in battle scenes, where combatants are constantly in and out, old texts seldom trouble to break up the scene: it is modern editors who are constantly imagining 'Another part of the Field.'" [104]

Spelling has been modernized. The basic copy's distinction between preterite endings in '*d* and '*ed* is preserved except where the elision of *e* occurs in the penultimate syllable; in such cases, the final syllable is contracted. Thus where Q reads "flattred," the present edition reads "flatter'd." Voiced preterites are indicated by a diacritical mark above the voiced syllable. *Then* and *I* have been silently emended to *Than* and *Aye*.

Punctuation has been brought into line with modern practice. Dashes are regularly used only to indicate interrupted speeches or shifts of address within a single speech.

References to stage directions in the notes are keyed decimally to the line of the text before or after which they occur. Thus, a note of 0.2 refers to the first line of the stage direction at the beginning of a scene, the scene designation being 0.1. A note on 12.1 refers to the first line of the stage direction following line 12 of the text of that particular scene.

The following abbreviations and short titles are employed in the textual notes. Details concerning the various editions may be found in the section on the text in the Introduction.

Q	-	quarto, 1605.
Steevens	-	*Six Old Plays*, 1779.
Hazlitt	-	Revision of J.P. Collier's *Shakespeare Library*, 1875.
MRS	-	*King Leir*, Malone Society Reprint, 1907.
Lee	-	*King Leir*, 1909.
Fischer	-	*Quellen zu Konig Lear*, 1914.
Bullough	-	*Narrative and Dramatic Sources of Shakespeare*, 1973.

+	-	subsequent editions agree.
SD	-	stage direction.
SP	-	speech prefix.

The following short titles are used in the explanatory notes:

Abbott	-	Abbott, E. A. *A Shakespearian Grammar*. 3rd ed., 1870; rpt. New York: Dover Publications, Inc., 1966.
Geneva	-	*The Geneva Bible: A Facsimile of the 1560 Edition.* intro. Lloyd E. Berry. Madison, Wisconsin: University of Wisconsin Press, 1969.
Nares	-	Nares, Robert. *A Glossary*, eds. James O. Halliwell and Thomas Wright. 2 vols. London, 1867.
Onions	-	Onions, C.T. *A Shakespeare Glossary*. 2nd ed., 1911; rpt. Oxford: Clarendon Press, 1951.
OED	-	*Oxford English Dictionary.* Oxford University Press, 1884-1928.
Tilley	-	Tilley, Morris Palmer. *A Dictionary of the Proverbs in England in the Sixteenth and Seventeenth Centuries*. Ann Arbor: University of Michigan Press, 1950.

FOOTNOTES

[1] Geoffrey Bullough, *Narrative and Dramatic Sources of Shakespeare* (London: Routledge and Kegan Paul, 1973), II, 271.

[2] *The Story of King Lear from Geoffrey of Monmouth to Shakespeare* (Berlin: Mayer and Muller, 1904).

[3] *Annals of English Drama 975-1700*, 2nd ed. (Philadelphia: University of Pennsylvania Press, 1964), p. 54.

[4] Henslowe, careless with his dating, entered the first performance as occurring on April 6, 1593, and the second on April 8, 1594. He knew that popularly the New Year began on January 1; "he also knew that legal and official documents, when they did not adopt the system of regnall years, reckoned by what is sometimes known as the Marian year, beginning on the feast of the Annunciation or Lady Day. He never made up his mind as to which convention he intended to follow, and lest he should be thought to commit himself to either, was not only in the habit of changing the date in his accounts at any time between 1 Jan. and 25 Mar., but frequently carried on the old date well into April, and sometimes even into May" (W.W. Greg, ed., *Henslowe's Diary* [London: A.H. Bullen, 1908], II, 46).

[5] R.A. Foakes and R.T. Rickert, edd., *Henslowe's Diary* (Cambridge: Cambridge University Press, 1961), p. 21.

[6] Edward Arber, ed., *A Transcript of the Registers of the Company of Stationers of London, 1554-1640* (London: [Privately printed], 1875-77), II, 649.

[7] W.W.Greg, "The Date of *King Lear* and Shakespeare's Use of Earlier Versions of the Story," *The Library*, 20 (1940), 378.

[8] Entering a play in the Register did not mean that the play would automatically be published. Of four other plays entered on the same day, only one, *The History of Friar Bacon and Friar Bungay*, seems to have been published the same year. The second, *David and Bethsaba*, exists only in an edition of 1599, while the other two, *Robin Hood* and *John of Gaunt*, are not known to have been printed at all ("The Date of *King Lear*," p. 378).

[9] *Ibid.*, p. 379.

[10] W.W. Greg, *Some Aspects and Problems of London Publishing Between 1550 and 1650*, (Oxford: Clarendon Press, 1956), p. 80.

[11] After Edward White's death in 1620 his widow continued her husband's printing trade. When she died, the copyrights of *Leir* and other publications were transferred to Edward Allde on June 29, 1624

(Arber, IV, 120). *Leir and his daughters* is listed in this transfer along with such works as *Friar Bacon and Friar Bungay, Arden of Feversham,* and *Euphues: His Censure to Philautus. King Leir* appears once again in the Stationers' Register on April 22, 1640. After the death of Allde's widow, Richard Olton, a son-in-law, inherited the copyright (Arber, IV, 507).

[12] "Essay on Chronological Order of Plays," *The Plays of William Shakespeare*, Second edition, rev. and augmented by Isaac Reed (London: C. Bathurst, 1778), II, 578.

[13] John P. Collier, *The Plays of Shakespeare* (London: Whittaker and Co., 1842-4), VII, 353; Henry N. Hudson, *The Works of Shakespeare* (Boston: J. Munroe and Co., 1851-7), IX, 391; Alexander Dyce, *The Works of Shakespeare* (London: Chapman and Hall, 1864-7), I, clxxxvi; Frederick Fleay, *A Chronicle History of the Life and Works of William Shakespeare, Player, Poet, and Play Maker* (London: J.C. Nimmo, 1886), p. 237.

[14] "The Date of *King Lear*," p. 383.

[15] F.C. Francis, "The Shakespeare Collection in the British Museum," *Shakespeare Survey*, 3 (1966), 45.

[16] The evidence for this inference is not overwhelming. A number of studies would need to be done in order to be more convincing in my argument, studies such as a thorough analysis of the appearances of various types throughout the book, the length of line, the headlines, and the press variants. But it is impossible for me to do more than rudimentary work on the text for the following reasons: (1) there are only four extant copies of the play; two are in the British Museum and the other two are in the Folger and Huntington libraries, so it is not possible to study these four texts simultaneously; and if it were, the small number of copies would not provide the amount of data necessary to reach reliable conclusions about the composition and imposition of the text. (2) I am also working from xeroxed copies made from microfilm of the texts. The copies are, therefore, not as clear as originals would be, and the distortions caused by photographing and reproducing would make many conclusions questionable. Nevertheless, because we know that setting by formes of Elizabethan and Jacobean books was not unusual, we can with some degree of confidence assume that at least some parts of *King Leir* were set by formes rather than consecutively. Charlton Hinman has demonstrated that setting by formes appears to have been a more common occurrence than had been previously thought. See his article, "Cast-Off Copy for the First Folio of Shakespeare," *Shakespeare Quarterly*, 6 (1955), 257-731; R.K. Turner, Jr., "The Composition of *The Insatiate Countess*," *Studies in Bibliography*, 12 (1959), 198-203; and George W. Williams, "Setting by Formes in Quarto Printing," *Studies in Bibliography*, 11 (1958), 39-53.

[17] George W. Williams has examined the texts of several works -- *Epicedium* (STC 12751), *The First Part of the Contention betwixt the Two Famous Houses of Yorke and Lancaster* (STC 26099), *Menechmi* (STC 20002), and *The Comicall Historie of Alphonsus, King of Aragon* (STC 12233) -- and demonstrates that while some parts of these works were set by formes, other parts were set seriatum; some were set outer forme first, while others were set inner forme first; and some sheets were machined outer forme first, while others were machined inner forme first ("Setting by Formes in Quarto Printing," *Studies in Bibliography*, 11 [1958], 39-53.

[18] For a full discussion of the procedures, see Charlton Hinman, "Principles Governing the Use of Variant Spellings as Evidence of Alternate Setting by Two Compositors," *The Library*, 21 (1941), 78-94.

[19] "Printing Methods and Textual Problems in *A Midsummer Night's Dream*, Q1," *Studies in Bibliography*, 15 (1962), 46.

[20] One might assume with one skeleton printing that the old page of type would have to be distributed (thereby replenishing the fonts) before another forme could be composed. But this apparently was not the procedure. Joseph Moxon points out in *Mechanick Exercises* that the skeleton form a wrought off forme was picked up piece by piece and reassembled around a new letterpress (pp. 327-8). Running titles were transferred by hand from one position to another. Fredson Bowers explains that the same skeleton was transferred to the fresh letterpress, instead of the letterpress being added to the undisturbed skeleton. He points out that the printer, having moved the skeleton to the new pages on the stone, left the old page of type undisturbed and ready for distribution on a special bench where it would be out of the way. ("Notes on Running-Titles as Bibliographical Evidence," *Library*, 4th ser. [1938], p. 319).

[21] "Analytical Bibliography and Shakespeare's Text," *Modern Philology*, 62 (1964), 55. See also Charlton Hinman, *The Printing and Proof-Reading of the First Folio of Shakespeare*, 2 (Oxford: Clarendon Press, 1963), 47-51. D.F. McKenzie, however, cautions that Turner's statement rests on the assumption that a printing house saw a single book through production before beginning another. He argues that "a smaller printing house, never using more than two presses, often one and a half, and occasionally only one, habitually printed several books concurrently." This meant not only "that several books were in production at the same time but that each workman, whether at press or case, was often engaged on several books more or less at once. ("Printers of the Mind: Some Notes on Bibliographical Theories and Printing-House Practices," *Studies in Bibliography*, 22 [1969], 14 ff., on concurrent printing).

[22] According to Williams, "not all substitutions point to the exhaustion of the proper character. . . . Occasionally the compositor, knowing that he would run short of a character, seems to have saved his characters for use in prominent locations or mixed his proper and improper sorts indiscriminately" (Setting by Formes in Quarto Printing," pp. 39-40).

[23] Williams points out that "distribution in the middle of a sheet is common" ("Setting by Formes in Quarto Printing, " p. 42n).

[24] "Date of *King Lear*," pp. 379-380.

[25] Wilfred Jewkes, *Act Division in Elizabethan and Jacobean Drama 1583-1616* (Hamden, Conn.: The Shoestring Press, 1958), p. 201.

[26] *Ibid.*, p.202.

[27] *The Library*, 12 (1931), 253-275.

[28] (Oxford: Clarendon Press, 1955), pp. 105-147.

[29] The 1605 quarto lacks the traits indicative of the author's foul papers: loose ends, false starts, and unresolved confusions in the text which sometimes reveal themselves as duplications in print; inconsistency in the designation of characters in directions and prefixes alike; occasionally the substitution of the name of an actor, when the part is written with a particular performer in mind; and the appearance occasionally of explanatory glosses on the text. Nor does the quarto show any of the

characteristics associated with a prompt-book: the marking of entries a few lines earlier than required by the action; repetitions of stage directions which would indicate that the book-keeper added his own to the playwright's; the appearance of actors' names duplicating those of characters in the play; and warning to the actors to be ready (*The Shakespeare First Folio*, p. 142).

[30] *The Shakespeare First Folio*, p. 124.

[31] (Cambridge: Cambridge University Press, 1915), p. 64.

[32] *The Shakespeare First Folio*, p. 122.

[33] *Ibid.*, p. 123.

[34] R.B. McKerrow, "The Elizabethan Printer and Dramatic Manuscripts," *The Library* 12 (1931), 270-272.

[35] Bullough, p. 272.

[36] (Berlin: Mayer and Muller, 1904).

[37] *Albion's England* first appeared in 1586. It is a history of England written in verse form recounting the national destiny from the beginning to the death of Henry VII. Subsequent editions were enlarged in 1589, 1592, 1596, and 1602 until it reached sixteen books in 1606 and came down to the reign of James I (C.S. Lewis, *English Literature in the Sixteenth Century Excluding Drama* [Oxford: Clarendon Press, 1944], p. 465).

[38] The first extant edition of *The Mirror for Magistrates* appeared in 1559. There were eight editions of the work, the last one appearing in 1587. In 1574, John Higgins had written a new work, published by Thomas Marsh, entitled:
> THE FIRST/ parte of the Mirour for/ Magistrates, containing the falles of the first/ infortunate Princes/ of this lande:/ From the comming of Brute/ to the incarnation of our/ Sauiour and redemer/ Iesu Christe.

It is called the first part because it deals with earlier periods than those touched on in previous editions.

The same year, 1574, another edition of the original *Mirror* was published under a new title, THE LAST *parte of the Mirour for Magistrates*, because of Higgins' publication earlier. And in 1575 Thomas Marshe, the printer, published another edition of Higgins' *Mirrour*. In 1587 Higgins' work (some of it re-written) was included in a new edition along with the work of the authors of the original *Mirror*. It is the 1587 edition that includes the material the playwright of *King Leir* used (*The Mirror for Magistrates*, ed. Lily B. Campbell [New York: Barnes and Noble, 1960], pp. 16-17. See also *Parts Added to The Mirror for Magistrates*, ed. Lily B. Campbell [Cambridge: Cambridge University Press, 1946]).

[39] Books I-III first appeared in 1590.

[40] The "Pide Bull" quarto is the name given to the first edition of *King Lear* (1608), published by Nathaniel Butter. The name comes from Butter's shop, located "at the sign of the Pide Bull," where the book was sold. The second edition of *King Lear* bears the imprint "Printed for Nathaniel Butter, 1608," but it was actually printed in 1619 by William Jaggard who altered the date in order to circumvent an order of 1619 which forbade the printing of the King's Men's plays without their consent.

41 Kenneth Muir, ed., *King Lear*, The Arden Shakespeare (Cambridge, Mass.: Vintage Books, 1959), p. xxii. All quotations in this text are from his edition.

42 "Date of *King Lear*," p. 383.

43 *The Complete Works of Shakespeare* (New York: Scott, Foresman and Co., 1951), p. 980.

44 "Date of *King Lear*," p. 382.

45 Muir, *King Lear*, p. xxii.

46 *The Third Earl of Southampton* (London: Routledge and Kegan, 1922).

47 "*King Lear* and the Annesley Case," in *Festscrift: Rudolf Stamm*, (Berne, Switzerland, 1969), pp. 43-50.

48 *Narrative and Dramatic Sources of Shakespeare*, VII, 271.

49 Muir, *King Lear*, p. xliii.

50 E.K. Chambers, *The Elizabethan Stage* (Oxford: The Clarendon Press, 1923), II, 114.

51 Foakes and Rickert, ed., *Henslowe's Diary*, p. 7.

52 Chambers, II, 114.

53 Chambers, II, 126, 198.

54 "Date of *King Lear*," p. 385.

55 *Ibid.*

56 *Narrative and Dramatic Sources*, VII, 270.

57 Muir, *King Lear*, p. xxxii.

58 *The Chronicle History of King Leir: The Original of Shakespeare's 'King Lear'* ed. Sidney Lee (New York: Duffield and Co., 1909), p. xviii.

59 *King Lear*, The Arden Shakespeare (New York, 1906).

60 "Date of *King Lear*."

61 Muir, *King Lear*.

62 "Date of *King Lear*," pp. 386-87.

63 *Ibid.*, pp. 387-88.

64 Muir, *King Lear*, pp. xxxi-xxxii.

65 "Date of *King Lear*," p. 388.

66 *Ibid.*, p.397.

67 Bullough, p. 277.

68 *William Shakespeare: The Complete Works*, ed. Alfred Harbage (Baltimore: Penguin Books, 1969), p. 1259.

69 *The Backgrounds of Shakespeare's Plays* (New York: American Book Co., 1950), p.272.

70 *Shakespeare and the Rival Traditions* (New York: Macmillan, 1952), p. 62.

71 J.W. Lever, ed., *Measure for Measure*, The Arden Shakespeare (London: Methuen and Co., 1965), p. xlvii.

72 *The Triple Bond*, ed. Joseph G. Price (University Park, Penn.: Pennsylvania State University Press, 1975), pp. 92-117.

73 Barton, p. 97.

74 Lever, *Measure for Measure*, p. xlvii.

75 Lewis Theobald, *Works of Shakespeare* (London: J. Browne, 1734), V, 217.

76 Edward Capell, *Mr. William Shakespeare His Comedies, Histories, and Tragedies* (London: Henry Hughes, 1767-68), I, 55.

77 *Ibid.*

78 *The History of English Dramatic Poetry* (London: J. Murray, 1831) III, 75.

79 *Pictorial Edition of the Works of Shakespeare* (New York: P.F. Collier, 1838), I, 391.

80 (London: Macmillan and Co., 1875), I, 417.

81 *Shakespeare's Predecessors in the English Drama* (London: Smith, Elder, 1884), p. 369.

[82] *Ibid.*

[83] Lee, *King Leir*, p. xviii.

[84] *The English Chronicle Play* (New York: Macmillan, 1902), pp. 174-75.

[85] *A New Variorum Edition of the Works of Shakespeare: King Lear* (Philadelphia: J. P. Lippincott Co., 1908), p. 384.

[86] Craig, p. 980.

[87] *The English History Play in the Age of Shakespeare* (London: Methuen and Co., 1965), p. 247.

[88] Bullough, p. 281.

[89] "Elements in the Composition of *King Lear*." *Studies in Philology* 30 (1933), 38.

[90] Bullough, p. 282.

[91] Schelling, p. 175.

[92] *Variorum Shakespeare*, p. 396.

[93] *Ibid.*, p. 398.

[94] Lee, p. xlii.

[95] Robert A. Law, "*King Leir* and *King Lear*: An Examination of the Two Plays," *Studies in Honor of T. W. Baldwin* (Urbana: University of Illinois Press, 1958), p. 123.

[96] *English Tragedy before Shakespeare*, trans. T.S. Dorsch (London: Methuen and Co., 1961), p. 205.

[97] "*King Leir* and *King Lear*," p. 123.

[98] George Steevens, ed., *Six Old Plays* (London: S. Leacroft, 1779), II, 377-464.

[99] W.C. Hazlitt, ed., *Shakespeare's Library*, 2nd ed. (London: Reeves and Turner, 1875), VI, 305-387.

[100] W.W. Greg, ed., *The History of King Leir 1605*, Malone Society Reprint (Oxford: Oxford University Press, 1907).

[101] Sidney Lee, ed., *The Chronicle History of King Leir: The Original of Shakespeare's 'King Lear,'* The Shakespeare Library, I. Gollancz, gen. ed. (New York: Duffield and Co., 1909).

[102] Rudolf Fischer, ed., *Quellen zu König Lear*, Shakespeares Quellen, A. Brandl, gen. ed. (Bonn: A. Marcus und E. Weber Verlag, 1914).

[103] VII (London: Routledge and Kegan Paul, 1973), 337-402.

[104] *The First Folio*, pp. 142-143n.

The True Chronicle History of King

Leir and His Three Daughters.

ACTUS I.

[Scene i]

Enter King Leir and Nobles [Skalliger, Perillus].

LEIR.

    Thus to our grief the obsequies perform'd

    Of our too late deceas'd and dearest queen

    Whose soul, I hope, possess'd of heavenly joys,

    Doth ride in triumph 'mongst the cherubins.

    Let us request your grave advice, my lords,   5

    For the disposing of our princely daughters,

    For whom our care is specially employ'd,

    As nature bindeth, to advance their states

    In royal marriage with some princely mates;

    For, wanting now their mother's good advice,   10

    Under whose government they have receiv'd

    A perfect pattern of a virtuous life,

    Left as it were a ship without a stern,

    Or silly sheep without a pastor's care.

    Although ourselves do dearly tender them,   15

    Yet are we ignorant of their affairs;

    For fathers best do know to govern sons,

    But daughters' steps the mother's counsel turns.

A son we want for to succeed our crown,
And course of time hath cancelled the date   20
Of further issue from our withered loins.
One foot already hangeth in the grave,
And age hath made deep furrows in my face.
The world of me, I of the world am weary,
And I would fain resign these earthly cares   25
And think upon the welfare of my soul,
Which by no better means may be effected
Than by resigning up the crown from me
In equal dowry to my daughters three.

SKALLIGER.

A worthy care, my liege, which well declares   30
The zeal you bare unto our quondam queen.
And since your grace hath licens'd me to speak,
I censure thus: your majesty knowing well
What several suitors your princely daughters have,
To make them each a jointer more or less,   35
As is their worth, to them that love profess--

LEIR.

No more, nor less, but even all alike
My zeal is fix'd, all fashion'd in one mould;
Wherefore unpartial shall my censure be,
Both old and young shall have alike for me.   40

NOBLEMAN.

    My gracious lord, I heartily do wish

    That God had lent you an heir indubitate

    Which might have set upon your royal throne

    When fates should loose the prison of your life,

    By whose succession all this doubt might cease   45

    And, as by you, by him we might have peace.

    But after-wishes ever come too late,

    And nothing can revoke the course of fate;

    Wherefore, my liege, my censure deems it best

    To match them with some of your neighbor kings   50

    Bord'ring within the bounds of Albion,

    By whose united friendship this our state

    May be protected 'gainst all foreign hate.

LEIR.

    Herein, my lords, your wishes sort with mine,

    And mine, I hope, do sort with heavenly powers;   55

    For at this instant two near-neighboring kings,

    Of Cornwall and of Cambria, motion love

    To my two daughters, Gonorill and Ragan.

    My youngest daughter, fair Cordella, vows

    No liking to a monarch, unless love allows.   60

    She is solicited by divers peers,

    But none of them her partial fancy hears.

    Yet, if my policy may her beguile,

>
> I'll match her to some king within this isle
>
> And so establish such a perfect peace 65
>
> As fortune's force shall ne'er prevail to cease.

PERILLUS.
> Of us and ours, your gracious care, my lord,
>
> Deserves an everlasting memory
>
> To be enroll'd in chronicles of fame
>
> By never-dying perpetuity. 70
>
> Yet to become so provident a prince,
>
> Lose not the title of a loving father;
>
> Do not force love, where fancy cannot dwell,
>
> Lest streams, being stopp'd, above the banks do swell.

LEIR.
> I am resolv'd, and even now my mind 75
>
> Doth meditate a sudden stratagem
>
> To try which of my daughters loves me best
>
> Which till I know, I cannot be in rest.
>
> This granted, when they jointly shall contend
>
> Each to exceed the other in their love, 80
>
> Then at the vantage will I take Cordella,
>
> Even as she doth protest she loves me best.
>
> I'll say, "Then, daughter, grant me one request:
>
> To show thou lovest me as thy sisters do,
>
> Accept a husband whom myself will woo." 85
>
> This said, she cannot well deny my suit,

> Although, poor soul, her senses will be mute.
>
> Then will I triumph in my policy
>
> And match her with a king of Brittany.

SKALLIGER [*Aside*].

> I'll to them before and bewray your secrecy. 90

PERILLUS [*Aside*].

> Thus fathers think their children to beguile,
>
> And oftentimes themselves do first repent
>
> When heavenly powers do frustrate their intent. *Exeunt.*

[Scene ii]

> *Enter Gonorill and Ragan.*

GONORILL.

> I marvel, Ragan, how you can endure
>
> To see that proud pert peat, our youngest sister,
>
> So slightly to account of us, her elders,
>
> As if we were no better than herself.
>
> We cannot have a quaint device so soon 5
>
> Or new-made fashion of our choice invention
>
> But, if she like it, she will have the same
>
> Or study newer to exceed us both.
>
> Besides, she is so nice and so demure,
>
> So sober, courteous, modest, and precise, 10
>
> That all the court hath work enough to do
>
> To talk how she exceedeth me and you.

RAGAN.

    What should I do? Would it were in my power

    To find a cure for this contagious ill!

    Some desperate medicine must be soon applied   15

    To dim the glory of her mounting fame;

    Else, ere't be long, she'll have both prick and praise,

    And we must be set by for working days.

    Do you not see what several choice of suitors

    She daily hath, and of the best degree?   20

    Say amongst all she hap to fancy one

    And have a husband whenas we have none;

    Why then, by right, to her we must give place,

    Though it be ne'er so much to our disgrace.

GONORILL.

    By my virginity, rather than she   25

    Shall have a husband before me,

    I'll marry one or other in his shirt;

    And yet I have made half a grant already

    Of my good will unto the king of Cornwall.

RAGAN.

    Swear not so deeply, sister.   30

    Here cometh my Lord Skalliger;

    Something his hasty coming doth import.

        Enter Skalliger.

SKALLIGER.
>   Sweet princesses, I am glad I met you here so luckily,
>   Having good news which doth concern you both
>   And craveth speedy expedition.   35

RAGAN.
>   For God's sake, tell us what it is, my lord;
>   I am with child until you utter it.

SKALLIGER.
>   Madam, to save your longing, this it is:
>   Your father in great secrecy today
>   Told me he means to marry you out of hand   40
>   Unto the noble Prince of Cambria;
>   You, Madam, to the King of Cornwall's grace;
>   Your younger sister he would fain bestow
>   Upon the rich King of Hibernia,
>   But that he doubts she hardly will consent,   45
>   For hitherto she ne'er could fancy him.
>   If she do yield, why then, between you three
>   He will divide his kingdom for your dowries.
>   But yet there is a further mystery
>   Which, so you will conceal, I will disclose.   50

GONORILL.
>   Whate'er thou speak'st to us, kind Skalliger,
>   Think that thou speak'st it only to thyself.

SKALLIGER.

>He earnestly desireth for to know
>Which of you three do bear most love to him,
>And on your loves he so extremely dotes 55
>As never any did, I think, before.
>He presently doth mean to send for you
>To be resolv'd of this tormenting doubt,
>And look whose answer pleaseth him the best,
>They shall have most unto their marriages. 60

RAGAN.

>Oh, that I had some pleasing mermaid's voice
>For to enchant his senseless senses with!

SKALLIGER.

>For he supposeth that Cordella will,
>Striving to go beyond you in her love,
>Promise to do whatever he desires; 65
>Then will he straight enjoin her for his sake
>The Hibernian king in marriage for to take.
>This is the sum of all I have to say;
>Which, being done, I humbly take my leave,
>Not doubting but your wisdoms will foresee 70
>What course will best unto your good agree.

GONORILL.

>Thanks, gentle Skalliger; thy kindness undeserved
>Shall not be unrequited, if we live.

Exit Skalliger.

RAGAN.

>Now have we fit occasion offer'd us

>To be reveng'd upon her, unperceiv'd.   75

GONORILL.

>Nay, our revenge we will inflict on her

>Shall be accounted piety in us.

>I will so flatter with my doting father

>As he was ne'er so flatter'd in his life.

>Nay, I will say that if it be his pleasure   80

>To match me to a beggar, I will yield,

>For why I know, whatever I do say,

>He means to match me with the Cornwall king.

RAGAN.

>I'll say the like, for I am well assured,

>Whate'er I say to please the old man's mind,   85

>Who dotes as if he were a child again,

>I shall enjoy the noble Cambrian prince.

>Only to feed his humour will suffice

>To say I am content with anyone

>Whom he'll appoint me. This will please him more   90

>Than e'er Apollo's music pleased Jove.

GONORILL.

>I smile to think in what a woeful plight

>Cordella will be when we answer thus,

>   For she will rather die than give consent
>   To join in marriage with the Irish king. 95
>   So will our father think she loveth him not,
>   Because she will not grant to his desire,
>   Which we will aggravate in such bitter terms
>   That he will soon convert his love to hate;
>   For he, you know, is always in extremes. 100

RAGAN.
>   Not all the world could lay a better plot;
>   I long till it be put in practice. *Exeunt.*

[Scene iii]

> *Enter Leir and Perillus.*

LEIR.
>   Perillus, go seek my daughters!
>   Will them immediately come and speak with me.

PERILLUS.
>   I will, my gracious lord. *Exit.*

LEIR.
>   Oh, what a combat feels my panting heart
>   'Twixt children's love and care of common weal! 5
>   How dear my daughters are unto my soul
>   None knows but He that knows my thoughts and secret deeds.
>   Ah, little do they know the dear regard
>   Wherein I hold their future state to come.
>   When they securely sleep on beds of down, 10

These aged eyes do watch for their behalf;

While they, like wantons, sport in youthful toys,

This throbbing heart is pierc'd with dire annoys.

As doth the sun exceed the smallest star,

So much the father's love exceeds the child's.   15

Yet my complaints are causeless, for the world

Affords not children more conformable.

And yet, methinks, my mind presageth still

I know not what, and yet I fear some ill.

Enter Perillus with the three daughters.

Well, here my daughters come. I have found out   20

A present means to rid me of this doubt.

GONORILL.

Our royal lord and father, in all duty

We come to know the tenor of your will,

Why you so hastily have sent for us.

LEIR.

Dear Gonorill, kind Ragan, sweet Cordella,   25

Ye flourishing branches of a kingly stock,

Sprung from a tree that once did flourish green,

Whose blossoms now are nipp'd with winter's frost,

And pale grim death doth wait upon my steps

And summons me unto his next assizes--   30

Therefore, dear daughters, as ye tender the safety

Of him that was the cause of your first being,

Resolve a doubt which much molests my mind:
Which of you three to me would prove most kind,
Which loves me most, and which at my request   35
Will soonest yield unto their father's hest?

GONORILL.
I hope my gracious father makes no doubt
Of any of his daughters' love to him;
Yet, for my part, to show my zeal to you
Which cannot be in windy words rehears'd,   40
I prize my love to you at such a rate,
I think my life inferior to my love.
Should you enjoin me for to tie a millstone
About my neck and leap into the sea,
At your command I willingly would do it.   45
Yea, for to do you good, I would ascend
The highest turret in all Brittany
And from the top, leap headlong to the ground.
Nay, more! Should you appoint me for to marry
The meanest vassal in the spacious world,   50
Without reply I would accomplish it.
In brief, command whatever you desire,
And if I fail, no favor I require.

LEIR.
Oh, how thy words revive my dying soul!

CORDELLA [*Aside*].

    Oh, how I do abhor this flattery! 55

LEIR.

    But what saith Ragan to her father's will?

RAGAN.

    Oh, that my simple utterance could suffice

    To tell the true intention of my heart,

    Which burns in zeal of duty to your grace

    And never can be quench'd but by desire 60

    To show the same in outward forwardness.

    Oh, that there were some other maid that durst

    But make a challenge of her love with me,

    I'd make her soon confess she never loved

    Her father half so well as I do you. 65

    Aye, then my deeds should prove in plainer case

    How much my zeal aboundeth to your grace.

    But for them all, let his one mean suffice;

    To ratify my love before your eyes,

    I have right noble suitors to my love,

    No worse than kings, and haply I love one; 70

    Yet would you have me make my choice anew,

    I'd bridle fancy and be rul'd by you.

LEIR.

    Did never Philomel sing so sweet a note?

CORDELLA. [*Aside*].

    Did never flatterer tell so false a tale? 75

LEIR.

    Speak now, Cordella; make my joys at full,

    And drop down nectar from thy honey lips.

CORDELLA.

    I cannot paint my duty forth in words;

    I hope my deeds shall make report for me.

    But look what love the child doth owe the father, 80

    The same to you I bear, my gracious lord.

GONORILL.

    Here is an answer answerless indeed!

    Were you my daughter, I should scarcely brook it.

RAGAN.

    Dost thou not blush, proud peacock as thou art,

    To make our father such a slight reply? 85

LEIR.

    Why, how now, minion, are you grown so proud?

    Doth our dear love make you thus peremptory?

    What, is your love become so small to us

    As that you scorn to tell us what it is?

    Do you love us as every child doth love 90

    Their father? True indeed, as some

    Who, by disobedience, short their father's days,

    And so would you! Some are so father-sick

>   That they make means to rid them from the world,
>
>   And so would you! Some are indifferent   95
>
>   Whether their aged parents live or die,
>
>   And so are you! But didst thou know, proud girl,
>
>   What care I had to foster thee to this,
>
>   Ah, then thou wouldst say as thy sisters do,
>
>   "Our life is less than love we owe to you."   100

CORDELLA.

>   Dear father, do not so mistake my words,
>
>   Nor my plain meaning be misconstrued;
>
>   My tongue was never used to flattery.

GONORILL.

>   You were not best say I flatter; if you do,
>
>   My deeds shall show I flatter not with you.   105
>
>   I love my father better than thou canst.

CORDELLA.

>   The praise were great spoke from another's mouth,
>
>   But it should seem your neighbors dwell far off.

RAGAN.

>   Nay, here is one that will confirm as much
>
>   As she hath said, both for myself and her;   110
>
>   I say thou dost not wish my father's good.

CORDELLA.

>   Dear father--

LEIR.
> Peace, bastard imp, no issue of King Leir!
>
> I will not hear thee speak one tittle more.
>
> Call not me father, if thou love thy life,   115
>
> Nor these thy sisters once presume to name.
>
> Look for no help henceforth from me nor mine;
>
> Shift as thou wilt and trust unto thyself.
>
> My kingdom will I equally divide
>
> 'Twixt thy two sisters to their royal dower,   120
>
> And will bestow them worthy their deserts.
>
> This done, because thou shalt not have the hope
>
> To have a child's part in the time to come,
>
> I presently will dispossess myself
>
> And set up these upon my princely throne.   125

GONORILL.
> I ever thought that pride would have a fall.

RAGAN.
> Plain dealing, sister; your beauty is so sheen,
>
> You need no dowry to make you be a queen.

> > *Exeunt Leir, Gonorill, Ragan.*

CORDELLA.
> Now whither, poor forsaken, shall I go,
>
> When mine own sisters triumph in my woe,   130
>
> But unto Him, which doth protect the just?
>
> In Him will poor Cordella put her trust.

These hands shall labor for to get my spending,

And so I'll live until my days have ending. [*Exit.*]

PERILLUS.

Oh, how I grieve to see my lord thus fond   135

To dote so much upon vain flattering words.

Ah, if he but with good advice had weighed

The hidden tenor of her humble speech.

Reason to rage should not have given place,

Nor poor Cordella suffer such disgrace. *Exit.*

[Scene iv]

Enter the Gallian King with Mumford and

three nobles more.

KING.

Dissuade me not, my lords; I am resolv'd

This next fair wind to sail for Brittany

In some disguise, to see if flying fame

Be not too prodigal in the wondrous praise

Of these three nymphs, the daughters of King Leir.   5

If present view do answer absent praise,

And eyes allow of what our ears have heard,

And Venus stand auspicious to my vows,

And fortune favor what I take in hand,

I will return seiz'd of as rich a prize   10

As Jason when he won the golden fleece.

MUMFORD.
>Heavens grant you may; the match were full of honor,
>And well beseeming the young Gallian king.
>I would your grace would favor me so much
>As make me partner of your pilgrimage. 15
>I long to see the gallant British dames
>And feed mine eyes upon their rare perfections,
>For till I know the contrary, I'll say
>Our dames in France are far more fair than they.

KING.
>Lord Mumford, you have saved me a labor 20
>In off'ring that which I did mean to ask,
>And I most willingly accept your company.
>Yet, first I will enjoin you to observe
>Some few conditions which I shall propose.

MUMFORD.
>So that you do not tie mine eyes for looking 25
>After the amorous glances of fair dames,
>So that you do not tie my tongue from speaking,
>My lips from kissing when occasion serves,
>My hands from congees, and my knees to bow
>To gallant girls (which were a task more hard 30
>Than flesh and blood is able to endure).
>Command what else you please, I rest content.

KING.

> To bind thee from a thing thou canst not leave
> Were but a mean to make thee seek it more,
> And therefore speak, look, kiss, salute for me;   35
> In these, myself am like to second thee.
> Now hear thy task: I charge thee from the time
> That first we set sail for the British shore
> To use no words of dignity to me,
> But in the friendliest manner that thou canst   40
> Make use of me as thy companion;
> For we will go disguis'd in palmers' weeds,
> That no man shall mistrust us what we are.

MUMFORD.

> If that be all, I'll fit your turn, I warrant you.
> I am some kin to the Blunts, and I think the blunt-   45
> est of all my kindred; therefore, if I be too blunt
> with you, thank yourself for praying me to be so.

KING.

> Thy pleasant company will make the way seem short.
> It resteth now that in my absence hence
> I do commit the government to you,   50
> My trusty lords and faithful counsellors.
> Time cutteth off the rest I have to say;
> The wind blows fair, and I must needs away.

NOBLES.

> Heavens send your voyage to as good effect
>
> As we your land do purpose to protect. *Exeunt.*   55

[Scene v]

> *Enter the King of Cornwall and his man, booted and spur-*
>
> *red, a riding wand and a letter in his [Cornwall's] hand.*

CORNWALL.

> But how far distant are we from the court?

SERVANT.

> Some twenty miles, my lord, or thereabouts.

CORNWALL.

> It seemeth to me twenty thousand miles;
>
> Yet hope I to be there within this hour.

SERVANT (*to himself*).

> Then are you like to ride alone for me.   5
>
> I think my lord is weary of his life.

CORNWALL.

> Sweet Gonorill, I long to see thy face
>
> Which has so kindly gratified my love.
>
> *Enter the King of Cambria and his man, booted and spur-*
>
> *red, a riding wand and a letter [in his (Cambria's) hand].*

CAMBRIA (*he looks on the letter*).

> Get a fresh horse; for by my soul I swear
>
> I am past patience longer to forbear   10
>
> The wished sight of my beloved mistress,

Dear Ragan, stay and comfort of my life.

SERVANT (*to himself*).

>Now what in God's name doth my lord intend?
>
>He thinks he ne'er shall come at's journey's end.
>
>I would he had old Daedalus' waxen wings   15
>
>That he might fly, so I might stay behind;
>
>For ere we get to Troynovant, I see,
>
>He quite will tire himself, his horse, and me.
>
>>*Cornwall and Cambria look one upon another and start*
>>
>>*to see each other there.*

CORNWALL.

>Brother of Cambria, we greet you well,
>
>As one whom here we little did expect.   20

CAMBRIA.

>Brother of Cornwall, met in happy time,
>
>I thought as much to have met with the Sultan of Persia
>
>As to have met you in this place, my lord.
>
>No doubt it is about some great affairs
>
>That makes you here so slenderly accompanied.   25

CORNWALL.

>To say the truth, my lord, it is no less;
>
>And for your part, some hasty wind of chance
>
>Hath blown you hither thus upon the sudden?

CAMBRIA.

>My lord, to break off further circumstances,

          For at this time I cannot brook delays,   30

          Tell you your reason, I will tell you mine.

CORNWALL.

          In faith, content, and therefore to be brief,

          For I am sure my haste's as great as yours,

          I am sent for to come unto King Leir,

          Who by these present letters promiseth   35

          His eldest daughter, lovely Gonorill,

          To me in marriage, and for present dowry

          The moiety of half his regiment.

          The lady's love I long ago possess'd,

          But until now I never had the father's.   40

CAMBRIA.

          You tell me wonders, yet I will relate

          Strange news, and henceforth we must brothers call.

          Witness these lines: his honorable age,

          Being weary of the troubles of his crown,

          His princely daughter Ragan will bestow   45

          On me in marriage with half his seigniories,

          Whom I would gladly have accepted of

          With the third part, her complements are such.

CORNWALL.

          If I have one half and you have the other,

          Then between us we must needs have the whole.

CAMBRIA.
> The hole! How mean you that? 'Zlood, I hope   50
> We shall have two holes between us.

CORNWALL.
> Why, the whole kingdom.

CAMBRIA.
> Aye, that's very true.

CORNWALL.
> What then is left for his third daughter's dowry,
> Lovely Cordella, whom the world admires?

CAMBRIA.
> 'Tis very strange; I know not what to think,   55
> Unless they mean to make a nun of her.

CORNWALL.
> 'Twere pity such rare beauty should be hid
> Within the compass of a cloister's wall;
> But howsoe'er, if Leir's words prove true,
> It will be good, my lord, for me and you.   60

CAMBRIA.
> Then let us haste all danger to prevent,
> For fear delays do alter his intent. *Exeunt.*

[Scene vi]

> *Enter Gonorill and Ragan.*

GONORILL.
> Sister, when did you see Cordella last,

> That pretty piece that thinks none good enough
>
> To speak to her because, sir-reverence,
>
> She hath a little beauty extraordinary?

RAGAN.
> Since time my father warn'd her from his presence, 5
>
> I never saw her that I can remember.
>
> God give her joy of her surpassing beauty;
>
> I think her dowry will be small enough.

GONORILL.
> I have incens'd my father so against her
>
> As he will never be reclaim'd again. 10

RAGAN.
> I was not much behind to do the like.

GONORILL.
> Faith, sister, what moves you to bear her such good will?

RAGAN.
> In truth, I think the same that moveth you,
>
> Because she doth surpass us both in beauty.

GONORILL.
> Beshrew your fingers, how right you can guess. 15
>
> I tell you true; it cuts me to the heart.

RAGAN.
> But we will keep her low enough, I warrant,
>
> And clip her wings for mounting up too high.

GONORILL.

    Whoever hath her shall have a rich marriage of her.

RAGAN.

    She were right fit to make a parson's wife,   20

    For they, men say, do love fair women well

    And many times do marry them with nothing.

GONORILL.

    With nothing! Marry, God forbid! Why, are there any such?

RAGAN.

    I mean, no money.

GONORILL.

    I cry you mercy, I mistook you much;   25

    And she is far too stately for the Church.

    She'll lay her husband's benefice on her back

    Even in one gown, if she may have her will.

RAGAN.

    In faith, poor soul, I pity her a little.

    Would she were less fair or more fortunate.   30

    Well, I think long until I see my Morgan,

    The gallant Prince of Cambria, here arrive.

GONORILL.

    And so do I until the Cornwall king

    Present himself to consummate my joys.

    Peace, here cometh my father.   35

        Enter Leir, Perillus, and others.

LEIR.
> Cease, good my lords, and sue not to reverse
> Our censure which is now irrevocable.
> We have dispatched letters of contract
> Unto the Kings of Cambria and of Cornwall.
> Our hand and seal will justify no less.   40
> Then do not so dishonor me, my lords,
> As to make shipwreck of our kingly word.
> I am as kind as is the pelican
> That kills itself to save her young ones' lives,
> And yet as jealous as the princely eagle   45
> That kills her young ones if they do but dazzle
> Upon the radiant splendor of the sun.
> Within this two days, I expect their coming.
>
> *Enter Kings of Cornwall and Cambria*
>
> But in good time they are arriv'd already.
> This haste of yours, my lords, doth testify   50
> The fervent love you bear unto my daughters,
> And think yourselves as welcome to King Leir
> As ever Priam's children were to him.

CORNWALL.
> My gracious lord, and father too, I hope,
> Pardon for that I made no greater haste;   55
> But were my horse as swift as was my will
> I long ere this had seen your majesty.

CAMBRIA.
>   No other 'scuse of absence can I frame
>   Than what my brother hath inform'd your grace.
>   For our undeserved welcome, we do vow   60
>   Perpetually to rest at your command.

CORNWALL.
>   But you, sweet love, illustrious Gonorill,
>   The regent and the sovereign of my soul,
>   Is Cornwall welcome to your excellency?

GONORILL.
>   As welcome as Leander was to Hero,   65
>   Or brave Aeneas to the Carthage queen.
>   So and more welcome is your grace to me.

CAMBRIA.
>   Oh, may my fortune prove no worse than his,
>   Since heavens do know my fancy is as much.
>   Dear Ragan, say if welcome unto thee;   70
>   All welcomes else will little comfort me.

RAGAN.
>   As gold is welcome to the covetous eyes,
>   As sleep is welcome to the traveler,
>   As is fresh water to sea-beaten men,
>   Or moisten'd showers unto the parched ground,   75
>   Or anything more welcomer than this,
>   So and more welcome lovely Morgan is.

LEIR.
>	What resteth then but that we consummate
>	The celebration of these nuptial rites?
>	My kingdom I do equally divide.	80
>	Princes, draw lots, and take your chance as falls.
>		*Then they draw lots.*
>	These I resign as freely unto you
>	As erst by true succession they were mine.
>	And here I do freely dispossess myself
>	And make you two my true adopted heirs.	85
>	Myself will sojourn with my son of Cornwall
>	And take me to my prayers and my beads.
>	I know my daughter Ragan will be sorry
>	Because I do not spend my days with her.
>	Would I were able to be with both at once;	90
>	They are the kindest girls in Christendom.

PERILLUS.
>	I have been silent all this while, my lord,
>	To see if any worthier than myself
>	Would once have spoke in poor Cordella's cause,
>	But love or fear ties silence to their tongues.	95
>	Oh, hear me speak for her, my gracious lord,
>	Whose deed have not deserv'd this ruthless doom,
>	As thus to disinherit her of all.

LEIR.
> Urge this no more, and if thou love thy life!
>
> I say she is no daughter that doth scorn   100
>
> To tell her father how she loveth him.
>
> Whoever speaketh hereof to me again,
>
> I will esteem him for my mortal foe.
>
> Come, let us in to celebrate with joy
>
> The happy nuptials of these lovely pairs.   105
>
> > *Exeunt omnes; manet Perillus.*

PERILLUS.
> Ah, who so blind as they that will not see
>
> The near approach of their own misery?
>
> Poor lady, I extremely pity her;
>
> And whilst I live, each drop of my heart-blood
>
> Will I strain forth to do her any good. *Exit.*   110

[Scene vii]

> > *Enter the Gallian king and Mumford, disguised*
> >
> > *like pilgrims.*

MUMFORD.
> My lord, how do you brook this British air?

KING.
> "My lord?" I told you of this foolish humor
>
> And bound you to the contrary, you know.

MUMFORD.
> Pardon me for once, my lord, I did forget.

KING.

    "My lord" again? Then let's have nothing else   5

    And so be ta'en for spies, and then 'tis well.

MUMFORD.

    'Swounds, I could bite my tongue in two for anger!

    For God's sake, name yourself some proper name.

KING.

    Call me Trosillus; I'll call thee Denapoll.

MUMFORD.

    Might I be made the monarch of the world,   10

    I could not hit upon these names, I swear.

KING.

    Then call me Will; I'll call thee Jack.

MUMFORD.

    Well, be it so, for I have well deserv'd to

    be call'd Jack.

KING.

    Stand close, for here a British lady cometh.   15

    Enter Cordella.

    A fairer creature ne'er mine eyes beheld.

CORDELLA [*to herself*].

    This is a day of joy unto my sisters,

    Wherein they both are married unto kings;

    And I, by birth as worthy as themselves,

    Am turn'd into the world to seek my fortune.   20

> How may I blame the fickle Queen of Chance
>
> That maketh me a pattern of her power?
>
> Ah, poor weak maid, whose imbecility
>
> Is far unable to endure these brunts!
>
> Oh, father Leir, how dost thou wrong thy child,
>
> Who always was obedient to thy will!   25
>
> But why accuse I Fortune and my father?
>
> No, no, it is the pleasure of my God,
>
> And I do willingly embrace the rod.

KING.
> It is no goddess, for she doth complain
>
> On Fortune and th'unkindness of her father.   30

CORDELLA.
> These costly robes, ill fitting my estate,
>
> I will exchange for other, meaner habit.

MUMFORD.
> Now if I had a kingdom in my hands, I would
>
> exchange it for a milkmaid's smock and petticoat
>
> that she and I might shift our clothes together.   35

CORDELLA.
> I will betake me to my thread and needle
>
> And earn my living with my fingers' ends.

MUMFORD.
> Oh brave! God willing, thou shalt have my custom!
>
> By sweet St. Denis, here I sadly swear

>>For all the shirts and nightgear that I wear. 40

CORDELLA.
>>I will profess and vow a maiden's life.

MUMFORD.
>>Then I protest thou shalt not have my custom.

KING.
>>I can forbear no longer for to speak;
>>For if I do, I think my heart will break. 45

MUMFORD.
>>'Sblood, Will, I hope you are not in love with my sempster.

KING.
>>I am in such a labyrinth of love,
>>As that I know not which way to get out.

MUMFORD.
>>You'll ne'er get out unless you first get in.

KING.
>>I prithee, Jack, cross not my passions! 50

MUMFORD.
>>Prithee, Will, to her and try her patience.
>>>[*They come forward*].

KING.
>>Thou fairest creature, whatsoe'er thou art,
>>That ever any mortal eyes beheld,
>>Vouchsafe to me, who have o'erheard thy woes,
>>To show the cause of these thy sad laments. 55

CORDELLA.

>Ah, pilgrims, what avails to show the cause,
>
>When there's no means to find a remedy?

KING.

>To utter grief doth ease a heart o'ercharg'd.

CORDELLA.

>To touch a sore doth aggravate the pain.

KING.

>The silly mouse, by virtue of her teeth, 60
>
>Releas'd the princely lion from the net.

CORDELLA.

>Kind palmer, which so much desir'st to hear
>
>The tragic tale of my unhappy youth,
>
>Know this in brief: I am the hapless daughter
>
>Of Leir, sometimes king of Brittany. 65

KING.

>Why, who debars his honorable age
>
>From being still the king of Brittany.

CORDELLA.

>None but himself hath dispossess'd himself,
>
>And given all his kingdom to the kings
>
>Of Cornwall and of Cambria with my sisters. 70

KING.

>Hath he given nothing to your lovely self?

CORDELLA.
> He lov'd me not and therefore gave me nothing,
> Only because I could not flatter him;
> And in this day of triumph to my sisters
> Doth Fortune triumph in my overthrow. 75

KING.
> Sweet lady, say there should come a king
> As good as either of your sisters' husbands
> To crave your love, would you accept of him?

CORDELLA.
> Oh, do not mock with those in misery;
> Nor do not think, though Fortune have the power 80
> To spoil mine honor and debase my state,
> That she hath any interest in my mind;
> For if the greatest monarch on the earth
> Should sue to me in this extremity,
> Except my heart could love and heart could like 85
> Better than any that I ever saw,
> His great estate no more should move my mind
> Than mountains move by blast of every wind.

KING.
> Think not, sweet nymph, 'tis holy palmer's guise
> To grieved souls fresh torments to devise; 90
> Therefore, in witness of my true intent,
> Let heaven and earth bear record of my words.

>   There is a young and lusty Gallian king,
>
>   So like to me as I am to myself,
>
>   That earnestly doth crave to have thy love   95
>
>   And join with thee in Hymen's sacred bonds.

CORDELLA.
>   The like to thee did ne'er these eyes behold.
>
>   Oh, live to add new torments to my grief.
>
>   Why didst thou thus entrap me unawares?
>
>   Ah, palmer, my estate doth not befit   100
>
>   A kingly marriage as the case now stands.
>
>   Whilom whenas I liv'd in honor's height,
>
>   A prince perhaps might postulate my love.
>
>   Now misery, dishonor, and disgrace
>
>   Hath light on me and quite revers'd the case.   105
>
>   Thy king will hold thee wise if thou surcease
>
>   The suit whereas no dowry will ensue.
>
>   Then be advised, palmer, what to do:
>
>   Cease for thy king, seek for thyself to woo.

KING.
>   Your birth's too high for any but a king.   110

CORDELLA.
>   My mind is low enough to love a palmer
>
>   Rather than any king upon the earth.

KING.
>   Oh, but you never can endure their life

Which is so strait and full of penury.

CORDELLA.
Oh, yes, I can, and happy if I might; 115
I'll hold thy palmer's staff within my hand
And think it is the scepter of a queen.
Sometime I'll set thy bonnet on my head
And think I wear a rich imperial crown.
Sometime I'll help thee in thy holy prayers 120
And think I am with thee in Paradise.
Thus I'll mock fortune as she mocketh me,
And never will my lovely choice repent;
For having thee, I shall have all content.

KING.
'Twere sin to hold her longer in suspense,
Since that my soul hath vow'd she shall be mine.-- 125
Ah, dear Cordella, cordial to my heart,
I am no palmer as I seem to be,
But hither come in this unknown disguise
To view th'admired beauty of those eyes. 130
I am the king of Gallia, gentle maid,
Although thus slenderly accompanied,
And yet thy vassal by imperious love,
And sworn to serve thee everlastingly.

CORDELLA.
Whate'er you be, of high or low descent, 135

All's one to me; I do request but this:
That as I am, you will accept of me,
And I will have you whatsoe'er you be.
Yet well I know you come of royal race;
I see such sparks of honor in your face. 140

MUMFORD.
Have palmers' weeds such power to win fair ladies?
Faith, then I hope the next that falls is mine.
Upon condition I no worse might speed,
I would forever wear a palmer's weed.
I like an honest and plain-dealing wench 145
That swears, without exceptions, "I will have you."
These foppets that know not whether to love a man or no
except they first go ask their mother's leave, by this
hand, I hate them ten times worse than poison.

KING.
What resteth then our happiness to procure? 150

MUMFORD.
Faith, go to church to make the matter sure.

KING.
It shall be so, because the world shall say
King Leir's three daughters were wedded in one day.
The celebration of this happy chance
We will defer until we come to France. 155

MUMFORD.

> I like the wooing that's not long a-doing.
>
> Well, for her sake, I know what I know:
>
> I'll never marry whilst I live, except I
>
> have one of these British ladies. My humour
>
> is alienated from the maids of France. *Exeunt.*

[Scene viii]

> *Enter Perillus, solus.*

PERILLUS.

> The king hath dispossess'd himself of all,
>
> Those to advance which scarce will give him thanks;
>
> His youngest daughter he hath turn'd away,
>
> And no man knows what is become of her.
>
> He sojourns now in Cornwall with the eldest,   5
>
> Who flatter'd him until she did obtain
>
> That at his hands which now she doth possess;
>
> And now she sees he hath no more to give,
>
> It grieves her heart to see her father live.
>
> Oh, whom should man trust in this wicked age   10
>
> When children thus against their parents rage?
>
> But he, the mirror of mild patience,
>
> Puts up all wrongs and never gives reply.
>
> Yet shames she not in most opprobrious sort
>
> To call him fool and dotard to his face,   15
>
> And sets her parasites of purpose oft

In scoffing wise to offer him disgrace.

Oh, iron age! Oh, times! Oh, monstrous, vild,

When parents are contemned of the child!

His pension she hath half restrain'd from him   20

And will ere long the other half, I fear;

For she thinks nothing is bestow'd in vain

But that which doth her father's life maintain.

Trust not alliance, but trust strangers rather,

Since daughters prove disloyal to the father.   25

Well, I will counsel him the best I can.

Would I were able to redress his wrong;

Yet what I can, unto my utmost power,

He shall be sure of to the latest hour. *Exit.*

[Scene ix]

Enter Gonorill and Skalliger.

GONORILL.

I prithee, Skalliger, tell me what thou think'st;

Could any woman of our dignity

Endure such quips and peremptory taunts

As I do daily from my doting father?

Doth't not suffice that I him keep of alms   5

Who is not able for to keep himself,

But, as if he were our better, he should think

To check and snap me up at every word?

I cannot make me a new-fashioned gown

    And set it forth with more than common cost,   10
    But his old doting, doltish, withered wit
    Is sure to give a senseless check for it.
    I cannot make a banquet extraordinary
    To grace myself and spread my name abroad,
    But he, old fool, is captious by and by,   15
    And saith the cost would well suffice for twice.
    Judge then, I pray, what reason is't that I
    Should stand alone charg'd with his vain expense,
    And that my sister Ragan should go free,
    To whom he gave as much as unto me?   20
    I prithee, Skalliger, tell me if thou know
    By any means to rid me of this woe.

SKALLIGER.
    Your many favors still bestow'd on me
    Bind me in duty to advise your grace
    How you may soonest remedy this ill.   25
    The large allowance which he hath from you
    Is that which makes him so forget himself;
    Therefore, abridge it half, and you shall see
    That having less, he will more thankful be,
    For why abundance maketh us forget   30
    The fountains whence the benefits do spring.

GONORILL.
    Well, Skalliger, for thy kind advice herein,

>I will not be ungrateful, if I live.
>
>I have restrained half his portion already,
>
>And I will presently restrain the other, 35
>
>That having no means to relieve himself,
>
>He may go seek elsewhere for better help. *Exit.*

SKALLIGER.
>Go, viperous woman, shame to all thy sex!
>
>The heavens no doubt will punish thee for this, 40
>
>And me a villain, that to curry favor
>
>Have given the daughter counsel 'gainst the father.
>
>But us the world doth this experience give:
>
>That he that cannot flatter cannot live. *Exit.*

[Scene x]

Enter King of Cornwall, Leir, Perillus, and Nobles.

CORNWALL.
>Father, what aileth you to be so sad?
>
>Methinks you frolic not as you were wont.

LEIR.
>The nearer we do grow unto our graves,
>
>The less we do delight in worldly joys.

CORNWALL.
>But if a man can frame himself to mirth, 5
>
>It is a mean for to prolong his life.

LEIR.
>Then welcome sorrow, Leir's only friend,

Who doth desire his troubled days had end.

CORNWALL.

Comfort yourself, father; here comes your daughter,

Who much will grieve, I know, to see you sad.   10

Enter Gonorill.

LEIR.

But more doth grieve, I fear, to see me live.

CORNWALL.

My Gonorill, you come in wished time

To put your father from these pensive dumps.

In faith, I fear that all things go not well.

GONORILL.

What, do you fear that I have anger'd him?   15

Hath he complain'd of me unto my lord?

I'll provide him a piece of bread and cheese,

For in a time he'll practice nothing else

Than carry tales from one unto another.

'Tis all his practice for to kindle strife   20

'Twixt you, my lord, and me, your loving wife;

But I will take an order, if I can,

To cease th'effect where first the cause began.

CORNWALL.

Sweet, be not angry in a partial cause;

He ne'er complain'd of thee in all his life.   25

Father, you must not weigh a woman's words.

LEIR.
>Alas, not I; poor soul, she breeds young bones.
>
>And that is it makes her so touchy, sure.

GONORILL.
>What, breeds young bones already! You will make
>
>An honest woman of me then, belike.   30
>
>Oh, vile old wretch! Whoever heard the like
>
>That seeketh thus his own child to defame?

CORNWALL.
>I cannot stay to hear this discord sound. *Exit.*

GONORILL.
>For anyone that loves your company,
>
>You may go pack, and seek some other place   35
>
>To sow the seed of discord and disgrace. *Exit.*

LEIR.
>Thus say or do the best that e'er I can,
>
>'Tis wrested straight into another sense.
>
>This punishment my heavy sins deserve,
>
>And more than this, ten thousand thousand times;   40
>
>Else aged Leir them could never find.
>
>Cruel to him to whom he hath been kind!
>
>Why do I overlive myself to see
>
>The course of nature quite revers'd in me?
>
>Ah, gentle Death, if ever any wight   45
>
>Did wish thy presence with a perfect zeal,

> Then come, I pray thee, even with all my heart,
> And end my sorrows with thy fatal dart.
>
> *He weeps.*

PERILLUS [*comes forward*].

> Ah, do not so disconsolate yourself,
> Nor dew your aged cheeks with wasting tears. 50

LEIR.

> What man art thou that takest any pity
> Upon the worthless state of old Leir?

PERILLUS.

> One who doth bear as great a share of grief
> As if it were my dearest father's case.

LEIR.

> Ah, good my friend, how ill art thou advis'd 55
> For to consort with miserable men.
> Go, learn to flatter where thou may'st in time
> Get favor 'mongst the mighty, and so climb;
> For now I am so poor and full of want
> As that I ne'er can recompense thy love. 60

PERILLUS.

> What's got by flattery doth not long endure,
> And men in favor live not most secure.
> My conscience tells me, if I should forsake you,
> I were the hateful'st excrement on the earth;
> Which well do know, in course of former time, 65

How good my lord hath been to me and mine.

LEIR.

Did I e'er raise thee higher than the rest

Of all thy ancestors which were before?

PERILLUS.

I ne'er did seek it, but by your good grace

I still enjoyed my own with quietness.   70

LEIR.

Did I e'er give thee living to increase

The due revenues which thy father left?

PERILLUS.

I had enough, my lord, and having that,

What should you need to give me any more?

LEIR.

Oh, did I ever dispossess myself   75

And give thee half my kingdom in good will?

PERILLUS.

Alas, my lord, there were no reason why

You should have such a thought to give it me.

LEIR.

Nay, if thou talk of reason, then be mute,

For with good reason I can thee confute.   80

If they, which first by nature's sacred law

Do owe to me the tribute of their lives;

If they, to whom I always have been kind

    And bountiful beyond comparison;
    If they, for whom I have undone myself   85
    And brought my age unto this extreme want,
    Do now reject, contemn, despise, abhor me,
    What reason moveth thee to sorrow for me?

PERILLUS.
    Where reason fails, let tears confirm my love,
    And speak how much your passions do me move.   90
    Ah, good my lord, condemn not all for one;
    You have two daughters left to whom I know
    You shall be welcome, if you please to go.

LEIR.
    Oh, how thy words add sorrow to my soul,
    To think of my unkindness to Cordella,   95
    Whom causeless I did dispossess of all
    Upon th'unkind suggestions of her sisters;
    And for her sake I think this heavy doom
    Is fall'n on me, and not without desert.
    Yet unto Ragan was I always kind   100
    And gave to her the half of all I had.
    It may be if I should to her repair,
    She would be kinder and entreat me fair,

PERILLUS.
    No doubt she would, and practice ere't be long
    By force of arms for to redress your wrong.   105

LEIR.
> Well, since thou dost advise me for to go,
>
> I am resolv'd to try the worst of woe. *Exeunt.*

[Scene xi]

> *Enter Ragan solus.*

RAGAN.
> How may I bless the hour of my nativity
>
> Which bodeth unto me such happy stars!
>
> How may I thank kind Fortune that vouchsafes
>
> To all my actions such desir'd event!
>
> I rule the King of Cambria as I please; 5
>
> The states are all obedient to my will,
>
> And look whate'er I say, it shall be so;
>
> Not anyone that dareth answer no.
>
> My eldest sister lives in royal state
>
> And wanteth nothing fitting her degree; 10
>
> Yet hath she such a cooling card withall
>
> As that her honey savoreth much of gall.
>
> My father with her is quartermaster still,
>
> And many times restrains her of her will.
>
> But if he were with me and serv'd me so, 15
>
> I'd send him packing somewhere else to go.
>
> I'd entertain him with such slender cost,
>
> That he should quickly wish to change his host. *Exit.*

[Scene xii]

Enter Cornwall, Gonorill, and attendants.

CORNWALL.
    Ah, Gonorill, what dire unhappy chance
    Hath sequester'd thy father from our presence
    That no report can yet be heard of him?
    Some great unkindness hath been offer'd him,
    Exceeding far the bounds of patience,   5
    Else all the world shall never me persuade
    He would forsake us without notice made.

GONORILL.
    Alas, my lord, whom doth it touch so near,
    Or who hath interest in this grief but I,
    Whom sorrow had brought to her longest home,   10
    But that I know his qualities so well?
    I know he is but stol'n upon my sister
    At unawares, to see her how she fares,
    And spend a little time with her to note
    How all things go and how she likes her choice;   15
    And when occasion serves, he'll steal from her
    And unawares return to us again.
    Therefore, my lord, be frolic and resolve
    To see my father here again ere long.

CORNWALL.
    I hope so too, but yet to be more sure,   20

I'll send a post immediately to know

Whether he be arrived there or no. *Exit.*

GONORILL.

    But I will intercept the messenger

    And temper him before he doth depart

    With sweet persuasions and with sound rewards,   25

    That his report shall ratify my speech

    And make my lord cease further to inquire.

    If he be not gone to my sister's court,

    As sure my mind presageth that he is,

    He haply may be traveling unknown ways,   30

    Fall sick, and as a common passenger,

    Be dead and buried. Would God it were so well,

    For then there were no more to do but this:

    He went away and none knows where he is.

    But say he be in Cambria with the king   35

    And there exclaim against me as he will;

    I know he is as welcome to my sister

    As water is into a broken ship.

    Well, after him I'll send such thunderclaps

    Of slander, scandal, and invented tales   40

    That all the blame shall be remov'd from me

    And, unperceiv'd, rebound upon himself.

    Thus with one nail another I'll expel,

    And make the world judge that I us'd him well.

Enter the messenger that should go to Cambria, with a letter in his hand.

GONORILL.

    My honest friend, whither away so fast?   45

MESSENGER.

    To Cambria, madam, with letters from the king.

GONORILL.

    To whom?

MESSENGER.

    Unto your father, if he be there.

GONORILL.

    Let me see them.

        She opens them.

MESSENGER.

    Madam, I hope your grace will stand between   50
me and my neck-verse, if I be call'd in
question for opening the king's letters.

GONORILL.

    'Twas I that opened them; it was not thou.

MESSENGER.

    Aye, but you need not care; and so must I, a
handsome man, be quickly truss'd up, and when   55
a man's hang'd, all the world cannot save him.

GONORILL.

    He that hangs thee were better hang his father,

Or that but hurts thee in the least degree;

I tell thee, we make great account of thee.

MESSENGER.

I am o'erjoy'd, I surfeit of sweet words; 60

Kind queen, had I a hundred lives, I would

Spend ninety-nine of them for you for that word.

GONORILL.

Aye, but thou would'st keep one life still,

And that's as many as thou art like to have.

MESSENGER.

That one life is not too dear for my good queen;

this sword, this buckler, this head, this heart, 65

these hands, arms, legs, tripes, bowels, and all

the members else whatsoever, are at your dispose;

use me, trust me, command me. If I fail in any-

thing, tie me to a dung cart and make a scaven-

ger's horse of me, and whip me so long as I have 70

any skin of my back.

GONORILL.

In token of further employment, take that.

Flings him a purse.

MESSENGER.

A strong bond, a firm obligation, good in law, good

in law; if I keep not the condition, let my neck be

the forfeiture of my negligience.

GONORILL.

    I like thee well; thou hast a good tongue.   75

MESSENGER.

    And as bad a tongue, if it be set on it, as any
oysterwife at Billinsgate hath; why, I have made
many of my neighbors forsake their houses with
railing upon them, and go dwell elsewhere; and
so by my means, houses have been good cheap in our   80
parish. My tongue, being well whetted with choler,
is more sharp than a razor of Palermo.

GONORILL.

    Oh, thou art a fit man for my purpose.

MESSENGER.

    Command me not, sweet queen, before you try me.
As my deserts are, so do think of me.   85

GONORILL.

    Well said. Then this is thy trial; instead of
carrying the king's letters to my father, carry
thou these letters to my sister, which contain
matter quite contrary to the other. There shall
she be given to understand that my father hath   90
detracted her, given out sland'rous speeches
against her, and that he hath most intolerably
abused me, set my lord and me at variance, and
made mutinies amongst the commons.

>   These things, although it be not so, 95
>
>   Yet thou must affirm them to be true
>
>   With oaths and protestations as will serve
>
>   To drive my sister out of love with him
>
>   And cause my will accomplished to be.
>
>   This do, thou winn'st my favor forever, 100
>
>   And makest a highway of preferment to thee
>
>   And all thy friends.

MESSENGER.

>   It sufficeth; conceit it is already done. I will
>
>   so tongue-whip him that I will leave him as bare
>
>   of credit as a poulter leaves a cony when she pulls 105
>
>   off his skin.

GONORILL.

>   Yet there is a further matter.

MESSENGER.

>   I thirst to hear it.

GONORILL.

>   If my sister thinketh convenient, as my letters
>
>   importeth, to make him away, hast thou the heart 110
>
>   to effect it?

MESSENGER.

>   Few words are best in so small a matter;
>
>   These are but trifles. By this book I will.
>
>   *Kiss the paper.*

GONORILL.

    About it presently, I long till it be done.

MESSENGER.

    I fly, I fly.   *Exeunt.*   115

[Scene xiii]

    Enter Cordella solus.

CORDELLA.

    I have been over-negligent today
    In going to the temple of my God
    To render thanks for all His benefits,
    Which He miraculously hath bestowed on me
    In raising me out of my mean estate,   5
    Whenas I was devoid of worldly friends,
    And placing me in such a sweet content
    As far exceeds the reach of my deserts.
    My kingly husband, mirror of his time
    For zeal, for justice, kindness, and for care   10
    To God his subjects, me and common weal,
    By His appointment was ordain'd for me.
    I cannot wish the thing that I do want;
    I cannot want the thing, but I may have
    Save only this which I shall ne'er obtain: 15
    My father's love. Oh, this I ne'er shall gain.
    I would abstain from any nutriment,
    And pine my body to the very bones.

> Barefoot I would on pilgrimage set forth
>
> Unto the furthest quarters of the earth,   20
>
> And all my lifetime would I sackcloth wear
>
> And, mourning-wise, pour dust upon my head,
>
> So he but to forgive me once would please,
>
> That his gray hairs might go to heaven in peace.
>
> And yet I know not how I him offended,   25
>
> Or wherein justly I have deserved blame.
>
> Oh sisters! You are much to blame in this.
>
> It was not he but you that did me wrong.
>
> Yet God forgive both him and you and me,
>
> Even as I do in perfect charity.   30
>
> I will to church and pray unto my Savior
>
> That, ere I die, I may obtain his favor. *Exit*.

[Scene xiv]

> *Enter Leir and Perillus, faintly.*

PERILLUS.

> Rest on me, my lord, and stay yourself;
>
> The way seems tedious to your aged limbs.

LEIR.

> Nay, rest on me, kind friend, and stay thyself;
>
> Thou art as old as I, but more kind.

PERILLUS.

> Ah, good my lord, it ill befits that I   5
>
> Should lean upon the person of a king.

LEIR.
>But it fits worse that I should bring thee forth,
>That had no cause to come along with me,
>Through these uncouth paths and tireful ways,
>And never ease thy fainting limbs a whit.   10
>Thou hast left all--aye, all--to come with me
>And I, for all, have nought to guerdon thee.

PERILLUS.
>Cease, good my lord, to aggravate my woes
>With these kind words, which cuts my heart in two
>To think your will should want the power to do.   15

LEIR.
>Cease, good Perillus, for to call me lord,
>And think me but the shadow of myself.

PERILLUS.
>That honorable title will I give
>Unto my lord so long as I do live.
>Oh, be of comfort, for I see the place   20
>Whereas your daughter keeps her residence.
>And lo, in happy time, to Cambrian prince
>Is here arriv'd to gratify our coming.

>>*Enter the Prince of Cambria, Ragan, and Nobles;*
>>*look upon them and whisper together.*

LEIR.
>Were I best speak, or sit me down and die?

I am asham'd to tell this heavy tale. 25

PERILLUS.

Then let me tell it, if you please, my lord;

'Tis shame for them that were the cause thereof.

CAMBRIA.

What two old men are those that seem so sad?

Methinks I should remember well their looks.

RAGAN. [*Aside*].

No I mistake not; sure it is my father. 30

I must dissemble kindness now of force.

She runneth to him and kneels down, saying:

Father, I bid you welcome, full of grief

To see your grace us'd thus unworthily

And ill befitting for your reverend age,

To come on foot a journey so indurable. 35

Oh, what disaster chance hath been the cause

To make your cheeks so hollow, spare, and lean?

He cannot speak for weeping. For God's love, come.

Let us refresh him with some needful things,

And at more leisure we may better know 40

Whence springs the ground of this unlook'd-for woe.

CAMBRIA.

Come father, ere we any further talk,

You shall refresh you after this weary walk.

Exeunt, manet Ragan.

RAGAN.

    Comes he to me with finger in the eye

    To tell a tale against my sister here   45

    Whom I do know he greatly hath abus'd?

    And now, like a contentious crafty wretch,

    He first begins for to complain himself,

    Whenas himself is in the greatest fault.

    I'll not be partial in my sister's cause.   50

    Nor yet believe his doting vain reports,

    Who for a trifle, safely I dare say,

    Upon a spleen is stolen thence away,

    And here, forsooth, he hopeth to have harbor

    And to be moan'd and made on like a child.   55

    But ere't be long, his coming he shall curse,

    And truly say he came from bad to worse.

    Yet will I make fair weather to procure

    Convenient means, and then I'll strike it sure. *Exit.*

[Scene xv]

    Enter Messenger solus.

MESSENGER.

    Now happily I am arrived here

    Before the stately palace of the Cambrian king.

    If Leir be here safe-seated and in rest,

    To rouse him from it I will do my best.

    Enter Ragan.

       Now, bags of gold, your virtue is, no doubt,   5

       To make me in my message bold and stout.--

       The King of Heaven preserve your majesty,

       And send your highness everlasting reign.

RAGAN.

       Thanks, good my friend; but what imports thy message?

MESSENGER.

       Kind greetings from the Cornwall queen;   10

       The residue these lettes will declare.

           She opens the letters.

RAGAN.

       How fares our royal sister?

MESSENGER.

       I did leave her at my parting in good health.

           She reads the letter, frowns, and stamps.

       See how her color comes and goes again,

       Now red as scarlet, now as pale as ash.   15

       See how she knits her brow and bites her lips

       And stamps and makes a dumb show of disdain,

       Mix'd with revenge and violent extremes.

       Here will be more work and more crowns for me.

RAGAN.

       Alas, poor soul, and hath he us'd her thus?   20

       And is he now come hither with intent

       To set divorce betwixt my lord and me?

Doth he give out that he doth hear report
That I do rule my husband as I list,
And therefore means to alter so the case   25
That I shall know my lord to be my head?
Well, it were best for him to take good heed,
Or I will make him hop without a head
For his presumption, dotard that he is.
In Cornwall he hath made such mutinies: 30
First, setting of the king against the queen,
Then stirring up the commons 'gainst the king,
That had he there continued any longer,
He had been call'd in question for his fact.
So upon that occasion thence he fled,   35
And comes thus slyly stealing unto us;
And now already since his coming hither
My lord and he are grown in such a league
That I can have no conference with his grace.
I fear he doth already intimate   40
Some forged cavillations 'gainst my state.
'Tis therefore best to cut him off in time,
Lest slanderous rumors once abroad dispers'd,
It is too late for them to be revers'd.--
Friend, as the tenor of these letters shows,   45
My sister puts great confidence in thee.

MESSENGER.
> She never yet committed trust to me
>
> But that, I hope, she found me always faithful;
>
> So will I be to any friend of hers
>
> That hath occasion to employ my help. 50

RAGAN.
> Hast thou the heart to act a stratagem,
>
> And give a stab or two if need require?

MESSENGER.
> I have a heart compact of adamant
>
> Which never knew what melting pity meant.
>
> I weigh no more the murd'ring of a man 55
>
> Than I respect the cracking of a flea
>
> When I do catch her biting on my skin.
>
> If you will have your husband or your father
>
> Or both of them sent to another world,
>
> Do but command me do't, it shall be done. 60

RAGAN.
> It is enough; we make no doubt of thee.
>
> Meet us tomorrow here at nine o'clock;
>
> > [*Gives him a purse.*]
>
> Meanwhile, farewell, and drink that for my sake. *Exit.*

MESSENGER.
> Aye, this is it will make me do the deed.
>
> Oh, had I every day such customers, 65

> This were the gainfull'st trade in Christendom!
>
> A purse of gold giv'n for a paltry stab!
>
> Why, here's a wench that longs to have a stab.
>
> Well, I could give it her and ne'er hurt her neither. [*Exit.*]

[Scene xvi]

Enter the Gallian king and Cordella.

KING.
> When will these clouds of sorrow once disperse
>
> And smiling joy triumph upon thy brow?
>
> When will this scene of sadness have an end
>
> And pleasant acts ensue to move delight?
>
> When will my lovely queen cease to lament   5
>
> And take some comfort to her grieved thoughts?
>
> If of thyself thou deign'st to have no care,
>
> Yet pity me whom thy grief makes despair.

CORDELLA.
> Oh, grieve not you, my lord; you have no cause.
>
> Let not my passions move your mind a whit,   10
>
> For I am bound by nature to lament
>
> For his ill will that life to me first lent.
>
> If so the stock be dried with disdain,
>
> Withered and sere the branch must needs remain.

KING.
> But thou art now graft in another stock.   15
>
> I am the stock and thou the lovely branch,

And from my root continual sap shall flow

To make thee flourish with perpetual spring.

Forget thy father and thy kindred now,

Since they forsake thee like inhuman beasts.   20

Think they are dead, since all their kindness dies,

And bury them where black oblivion lies.

Think not thou art the daughter of old Leir,

Who did unkindly disinherit thee,

But think thou art the noble Gallian queen   25

And wife to him that dearly loveth thee.

Embrace the joys that present with thee dwell;

Let sorrow pack and hide herself in hell.

CORDELLA.

Not that I miss my country or my kin,

My old acquaintance or my ancient friends,   30

Doth any whit distemperate my mind,

Knowing you, which are more dear to me

Than country, kin, and all things else can be;

Yet pardon me, my gracious lord, in this,

For what can stop the course of nature's power?   35

As easy is it for four-footed beasts

To stay themselves upon the liquid air

And mount aloft into the element

And overstrip the feathered fowls in flight.

As easy is it for the slimy fish   40

> To live and thrive without the help of water;
> As easy is it for the blackamoor
> To wash the tawny color from his skin,--
> Which all oppose against the course of nature,--
> As I am able to forget my father. 45

KING.
> Mirror of virtue. Phoenix of our age!
> Too kind a daughter for an unkind father!
> Be of good comfort, for I will dispatch
> Ambassadors immediately for Brittayne
> Unto the king of Cornwall's court, whereat 50
> Your father keepeth now his residence
> And in the kindest manner him entreat
> That, setting former grievances apart,
> He will be pleas'd to come and visit us.
> If no entreaty will suffice the turn, 55
> I'll offer him the half of all my crown.
> If that moves not, we'll furnish out a fleet
> And sail to Cornwall for to visit him,
> And there you shall be firmly reconcil'd
> In perfect love as erst you were before. 60

CORDELLA.
> Where tongue cannot sufficient thanks afford,
> The King of Heaven remunerate my lord.

KING.

    Only be blithe, and frolic, sweet, with me;

    This and much more I'll do to comfort thee

                    [*Exeunt.*]

[Scene xvii]

        Enter Messenger solus.

MESSENGER.

    It is a world to see, now I am flush,

    How many friends I purchase everywhere!

    How many seeks to creep into my favor,

    And kiss their hands and bend their knees to me!

    No more, here comes the queen; now shall I know her mind   5

    And hope for to derive more crowns from her.

        Enter Ragan.

RAGAN.

    My friend, I see thou mind'st thy promise well

    And art before me here, methinks, today.

MESSENGER.

    I am a poor man, and it like your grace,

    But yet I always love to keep my word.   10

RAGAN.

    Well, keep thy word with me, and thou shalt see

    That, of a poor man, I will make thee rich.

MESSENGER.

    I long to hear it; it might have been dispatch'd,

If you had told me of it yesternight.

RAGAN.

It is a thing of right strange consequence,   15

And well I cannot utter it in words.

MESSENGER.

It is more strange that I am not by this

Beside myself with longing for to hear it.

Were it to meet the devil in his den

And try a bout with him for a scratch'd face,   20

I'd undertake it, if you would but bid me.

RAGAN.

Ah, good my friend, that I should have thee do

Is such a thing as I do shame to speak;

Yet it must needs be done.

MESSENGER.

I'll speak it for thee, queen; shall I kill thy father?   25

I know 'tis that, and if it be so, say.

RAGAN.

Aye.

MESSENGER.

Why, that's enough.

RAGAN.

And yet that is not all.

MESSENGER.

What else?

RAGAN.

>Thou must kill that old man that came with him. 30

MESSENGER.

>Here are two hands; for each of them is one.

RAGAN.

>And for each hand, here is a recompense.
>
>*Give him two purses.*

MESSENGER.

>Oh, that I have ten hands by miracle;
>
>I could tear ten in pieces with my teeth,
>
>So in my mouth you'd put a purse of gold. 35
>
>But in what manner must it be effected?

RAGAN.

>Tomorrow morning, ere the break of day,
>
>I, by a wile, will send them to the thicket
>
>That is about some two miles from the court,
>
>And promise them to meet them there myself, 40
>
>Because I must have some private conference
>
>About some news I have receiv'd from Cornwall.
>
>This is enough; I know they will not fail,
>
>And then be ready for to play thy part;
>
>Which done, thou may'st right easily escape, 45
>
>And no man once mistrust thee for the fact.
>
>But yet before thou prosecute the act,
>
>Show him the letter which my sister sent;

>There let him read his own indictment first,
>
>And then proceed to execution. 50
>
>But see thou faint not, for they will speak fair.

MESSENGER.
>Could he speak words as pleasing as the pipe
>
>Of Mercury, which charm'd the hundred eyes
>
>Of watchful Argus and enforc'd him sleep,
>
>>*To the purse.*
>
>Yet here are words so pleasing to my thoughts 55
>
>As quite shall take away the sound of his. *Exit.*

RAGAN.
>About it then, and when thou hast dispatch'd,
>
>I'll find a means to send thee after him. *Exit.*

[Scene xviii]

>*Enter Cornwall and Gonorill.*

CORNWALL.
>I wonder that the messenger doth stay
>
>Whom we dispatch'd for Cambria so long since.
>
>If that his answer do not please us well,
>
>And he do show good reason for delay,
>
>I'll teach him how to dally with his king, 5
>
>And to detain us in such long suspense.

GONORILL.
>My lord, I think the reason may be this:
>
>My father means to come along with him

    And therefor 'tis his pleasure he shall stay,

    For to attend upon him on the way.   10

CORNWALL.

    It may be so, and therefore till I know

    The truth thereof I will suspend my judgment.

        Enter Servant.

SERVANT.

    And't like your grace, there is an ambassador

    Arrived from Gallia and craves admittance to your majesty.

CORNWALL.

    From Gallia? What should his message   15

    Hither import? Is not your father happely

    Gone thither? Well, whatsoe'er it be,

    Bid him come in; he shall have audience.

        Enter Ambassador.

    What news from Gallia? Speak, ambassador.

AMBASSADOR.

    The noble king and queen of Gallia first salutes   20

    By me their honorable father, my lord Leir.

    Next, they command them kindly to your graces

    As those whose welfare they entirely wish.

    Letters I have to deliver to my lord Leir,

    And presents too, if I might speak with him.   25

GONORILL.

    If you might speak with him? Why do you think

We are afraid that you should speak with him?

AMBASSADOR.

    Pardon me, madam, for I think not so,

    But say so only 'cause he is not here.

CORNWALL.

    Indeed, my friend, upon some urgent cause   30

    He is at this time absent from the court;

    But if a day or two you here repose,

    'Tis very likely you shall have him here,

    Or else have certain notice where he is.

GONORILL.

    Are not we worthy to receive your message?   35

AMBASSADOR.

    I had in charge to do it to himself.

GONORILL. [*Aside*].

    It may be then 'twill not be done in haste.

    How doth my sister brook the air of France?

AMBASSADOR.

    Exceeding well, and never sick one hour

    Since first she set her foot upon the shore.   40

GONORILL.

    I am the more sorry.

AMBASSADOR.

                I hope not so, madam.

GONORILL.

    Didst thou not say that she was ever sick

    Since the first hour that she arrived there?

AMBASSADOR.

    No, madam, I said quite contrary.

GONORILL.

    Then I mistook thee.   45

CORNWALL.

    Then she is merry, if she have her health.

AMBASSADOR.

    Oh no, her grief exceeds until the time

    That she be reconcil'd unto her father.

GONORILL.

    God continue it.

AMBASSADOR.

                    What, madam?

GONORILL.

                          Why, her health.

AMBASSADOR.

    Amen to that; but God release her grief,   50

    And send her father in a better mind,

    Than to continue always so unkind.

CORNWALL.

    I'll be a mediator in her cause,

    And seek all means to expiate his wrath.

AMBASSADOR.

    Madam, I hope your grace will do the like.   55

GONORILL.

    Should I be a mean to exasperate his wrath

    Against my sister whom I love so dear? No, no.

AMBASSADOR.

    To expiate or mitigate his wrath,

    For he hath misconceived without a cause.

GONORILL.

    Oh, aye, what else?   60

AMBASSADOR.

    'Tis pity it should be so; would it were otherwise.

GONORILL.

    It were great pity it should be otherwise.

AMBASSADOR.

    Than how, Madam?

GONORILL.

    Than that they should be reconcil'd again.

AMBASSADOR.

    It shows you bear an honorable mind.   65

GONORILL *(speaks to herself)*.

    It shows thy understanding to be blind,

    And that thou had'st need of an interpreter.

    Well, I will know thy message ere't be long,

    And find a mean to cross it, if I can.

CORNWALL.
> Come in, my friend, and frolic in our court 70
> Till certain notice of my father come.

Exeunt.

[Scene xix]

Enter Leir and Perillus [with small bags].

PERILLUS.
> My lord, you are up today before your hour.
> 'Tis news to you to be abroad so rathe.

LEIR.
> 'Tis news indeed; I am so extreme heavy
> That I can scarcely keep my eyelids open.

PERILLUS.
> And so am I, but I impute the cause 5
> To rising sooner than we use to do.

LEIR.
> Hither my daughter means to come disguis'd;
> I'll sit me down and read until she come.

Pull out a book [from bag] and sit down.

PERILLUS.
> She'll not be long, I warrant you, my lord.
> But say a couple of these they call "good fellows" 10
> Should step out of a hedge and set upon us,
> We were in good case for to answer them.

LEIR.

>'Twere not for us to stand upon our hands.

PERILLUS.

>I fear we scant should stand upon our legs.

>But how should we do to defend ourselves? 15

LEIR.

>Even pray to God to bless us from their hands,

>For fervent prayer much ill hap withstands.

PERILLUS.

>I'll sit and pray with you for company;

>Yet was I ne'er so heavy in my life.

>>*They fall both asleep.*
>>*Enter the messenger or murderer with two*
>>>*daggers in his hands.*

MESSENGER.

>Were it not a mad jest if two or three of my 20
>profession should meet me and lay me down in a
>ditch and play rob-thief with me and perforce
>take my gold away from me, whilest
>I act this stratagem, and by this means the gray-
>beards should escape? Faith, when I were at liberty
>again, I would make no more to do but go to the next
>tree and there hang myself. 25

>>*See them and start.*

>But stay, methinks my youths are here already

And, with pure zeal, have prayed themselves asleep.

I think they know to what intent they came.

And are provided for another world.

    He takes their books away.

Now could I stab them bravely while they sleep,   30

And in a manner put them to no pain;

And doing so, I showed them mighty friendship,

For fear of death is worse than death itself;

But that my sweet queen will'd me for to show

This letter to them ere I did the deed.   35

Mass, they begin to stir. I'll stand aside;

So shall I come upon them unawares.

    They wake and rise.

LEIR.

I marvel that my daughter stays so long.

PERILLUS.

I fear we did mistake the place, my lord.

LEIR.

God grant we do not miscarry in the place.   40

I had a short nap, but so full of dread

As much amazeth me to think thereof.

PERILLUS.

Fear not, my lord; dreams are but fantasies

And slight imaginations of the brain.

MESSENGER [*Aside*].
>Persuade him so, but I'll make him and you 45
>Confess that dreams do often prove too true.

PERILLUS.
>I pray, my lord, what was the effect of it?
>I may go near to guess what it pretends.

MESSENGER [*Aside*].
>Leave that to me; I will expound the dream.

LEIR.
>Methought my daughters, Gonorill and Ragan, 50
>Stood both before me with such grim aspects,
>Each brandishing a falchion in their hands,
>Ready to lop a limb off where it fell;
>And in their other hands a naked poniard,
>Wherewith they stabb'd me in a hundred places, 55
>And to their thinking left me there for dead.
>But then my youngest daughter, fair Cordella.
>Came with box of balsam in her hand
>And poured it into my bleeding wounds,
>By whose good means I was recovered well, 60
>In perfect health as erst I was before;
>And with the fear of this, I did awake,
>And yet for fear, my feeble joints do quake.

MESSENGER [*Aside*].
>I'll make you quake for something presently.--

        [*Coming forward.*] Stand, Stand!   65

          They reel.

LEIR.

    We do, my friend, although with much ado.

MESSENGER.

    Deliver, deliver!

PERILLUS.

    Deliver us, good Lord, from such as he.

MESSENGER.

    You should have prayed before while it was time,

    And then perhaps you might have 'scap'd my hands;   70

    But you, like faithful watchmen, fell asleep

    The whilst I came and took your halberds from you,

        Show their books.

    And now you want your weapons of defense.

    How have you any hope to be delivered?

    This comes because you have no better stay   75

    But fall asleep when you should watch and pray.

LEIR.

    My friend, thou seem'st to be a proper man.

MESSENGER.

    'Sblood, how the old slave claws me by the elbow;

    He thinks belike to 'scape by scraping thus.

PERILLUS.

    And it may be, are in some need of money.   80

MESSENGER.

>That to be false, behold my evidence.

>>*Shows his purses.*

LEIR.

>If that I have will do thee any good,

>I give it thee even with a right good will.

>>*Take it.*

PERILLUS.

>Here, take mine too, and wish with all my heart,

>To do thee pleasure, it were twice as much. 85

>>*Take his and weigh them both in his hands.*

MESSENGER.

>I'll none of them; they are too light for me.

>>*Puts them in his pocket.*

LEIR.

>Why then, farewell; and if thou have occasion

>In anything to use me to the queen,

>'Tis like enough that I can pleasure thee.

>>*They proffer to go.*

MESSENGER.

>Do you hear, do you hear, sir? 90

>If I had occasion to use you to the queen,

>Would you do one thing for me I should ask?

LEIR.

>Aye, anything that lies within my power.

Here is my hand upon it. So, farewell.

Proffer to go.

MESSENGER.

Hear you, sir, hear you; pray, a word with you. 95

Methinks a comely honest ancient man

Should not dissemble with one for a vantage.

I know, when I shall come to try this gear,

You will recant from all that you have said.

PERILLUS.

Mistrust not him, but try him when thou wilt; 100

He is her father, therefore may do much.

MESSENGER.

I know he is, and therefore mean to try him.

You are his friend too; I must try you both.

AMBO.

Prithee do, prithee do.

Proffer to go out.

MESSENGER.

Stay, gray-beards then, and prove men of your words. 105

The queen hath tied me by a solemn oath

Here in this place to see you both dispatch'd;

Now for the safeguard of my conscience,

Do me the pleasure for to kill yourselves.

So shall you save me labor for to do it 110

And prove yourselves true old men of your words.

And here I vow, in sight of all the world,

I ne'er will trouble you, whilst I live, again.

LEIR.

Affright us not with terror, good my friend,

Nor strike such fear into our aged hearts; 115

Play not the cat which dallieth with the mouse,

And on a sudden maketh her a prey;

But if thou art mark'd for the man of death

To me and to my Damon, tell me plain,

That we may be prepared for the stroke 120

And make ourselves fit for the world to come.

MESSENGER.

I am the last of any mortal race

That e'er your eyes are likely to behold;

And hither sent of purpose to this place

To give a final period to your days, 125

Which are so wicked and have lived so long

That your own children seek to short your life.

LEIR.

Cam'st thou from France of purpose to do this?

MESSENGER.

From France? 'Zoons, do I look like a Frenchman?

Sure I have not mine own face on; somebody hath 130

chang'd faces with me and I know not of it. But

I am sure my apparel is all English. Sirrah, what

meanest thou to ask that question? I could spoil

the fashion of this face for anger. A French face!

LEIR.

Because my daughter, whom I have offended 135

And at whose hands I have deserv'd as ill

As ever any father did of child,

Is Queen of France--no thanks at all to me,

But unto God, who my injustice see.

If it be so that she doth seek revenge, 140

As with good reason she may justly do,

I will most willingly resign my life,

A sacrifice to mitigate her ire.

I never will entreat thee to forgive,

Because I am unworthy for to live. 145

Therefore, speak soon, and I will soon make speed,

Whether Cordella will'd thee do this deed.

MESSENGER.

As I am a perfect gentleman, thou speak'st French to me;

I never heard Cordella's name before,

Nor never was in France in all my life. 150

I never knew thou had'st a daughter there

To whom thou didst prove so unkind a churl;

But thy own tongue declares that thou hast been

A vile old wretch and full of heinous sin.

LEIR.
>   Ah no, my friend, thou are deceived much.   155
>   For her except, whom I confess I wrong'd
>   Through doting frenzy and o'erjealous love,
>   There lives not any under heaven's bright eye
>   That can convict me of impiety.
>   And, therefore, sure thou dost mistake the mark,   160
>   For I am in true peace with all the world.

MESSENGER.
>   You are the fitter for the King of Heaven;
>   And, therefore, for to rid thee of suspense,
>   Know thou the Queens of Cambria and Cornwall,
>   Thy own two daughters, Gonorill and Ragan,   165
>   Appointed me to massacre thee here.
>   Why would'st thou then persuade me that thou art
>   In charity with all the world? But now,
>   When thy own issue hold thee in such hate
>   That they have hired me t'abridge thy fate?   170
>   Oh, fie upon such vile dissembling breath
>   That would deceive even at the point of death;

PERILLUS.
>   Am I awake or is it but a dream?

MESSENGER.
>   Fear nothing, man, thou art but in a dream,
>   And thou shalt never wake until doomsday.   175

       By then, I hope thou wilt have slept enough.

LEIR.

       Yet, gentle friend, grant one thing ere I die.

MESSENGER.

       I'll grant you anything except your lives.

LEIR.

       Oh, but assure me by some certain token

       That my two daughters hired them to this deed.   180

       If I were once resolv'd of that, then I

       Would wish no longer life, but crave to die.

MESSENGER.

       That to be true, in sight of heaven, I swear.

LEIR.

       Swear not by heaven, for fear of punishment.

       The heavens are guiltless of such heinous acts.   185

MESSENGER.

       I swear by earth, the mother of us all.

LEIR.

       Swear not by earth, for she abhors to bear

       Such bastards as are murderers of her sons.

MESSENGER.

       Why then, by hell and all the devils I swear.

LEIR.

       Swear not by hell, for that stands gaping wide   190

       To swallow thee and if thou do this deed.

Thunder and lightning.

MESSENGER [*Aside*].

    I would that word were in his belly again;

    It hath frighted me even to the very heart.

    This old man is some strong magician;

    His words have turn'd my mind from this exploit.--   195

        [*to them.*]

    Then neither heaven, earth, nor hell be witness,

    But let this paper witness for them all.

        Shows Gonorill's letter.

    Shall I relent, or shall I prosecute?

    Shall I resolve, or were I best recant?

    I will not crack my credit with two queens   200

    To whom I have already pass'd my word.

    Oh, but my conscience for this act doth tell

    I get heaven's hate, earth's scorn, and pains of hell.

        They bless themselves.

PERILLUS.

    Oh just Jehovah, whose almighty power

    Doth govern all things in this spacious world,   205

    How canst thou suffer such outrageous acts

    To be committed without just revenge?

    Oh viperous generation and accurs'd,

    To seek his blood whose blood did make them first!

LEIR.
>   Ah, my true friend in all extremity,   210
>   Let us submit us to the will of God,
>   Things past all sense, let us not seek to know;
>   It is God's will, and therefore must be so.
>   My friend, I am prepared for the stroke.
>   Strike when thou wilt, and I forgive thee here,   215
>   Even from the very bottom of my heart.

MESSENGER.
>   But I am not prepared for to strike.

LEIR.
>   Farewell Perillus, even the truest friend
>   That ever lived in adversity;
>   The latest kindness I'll request of thee   220
>   Is that thou go unto my daughter, Cordella,
>   And carry her her father's latest blessing.
>   Withal desire her that she will forgive me,
>   For I have wrong'd her without any cause.
>   Now, Lord, receive me; for I come to thee,   225
>   And die, I hope, in perfect charity.
>   Dispatch, I pray thee; I have lived too long.

MESSENGER.
>   Aye, but you are unwise to send an errand
>   By him that never meaneth to deliver it.
>   Why, he must go along with you to heaven;   230

It were not good you should go all alone.

LEIR.

No doubt he shall, when by the course of nature

He must surrender up his due to death;

But that time shall not come till God permit.

MESSENGER.

Nay, presently, to bear you company.   235

I have a passport for him in my pocket,

Already seal'd, and he must needs ride post.

Show a bag of money.

LEIR.

The letter which I read imports not so;

It only toucheth me, no word of him.

MESSENGER.

Aye, but the queen commands it must be so,   240

And I am paid for him as well as you.

PERILLUS.

I, who have borne you company in life,

Most willingly will bear a share in death.

It skilleth not for me, my friend, a whit,

Nor for a hundred such as thou and I.   245

MESSENGER.

Marry, but it doth, sir, by your leave; your good

days are past. Though it be no matter for you,

'tis a matter for me; proper men are not so rife.

PERILLUS.
> Oh, but beware how thou dost lay thy hand
> Upon the high anointed of the Lord. 250
> Oh, be advised ere thou dost begin;
> Dispatch me straight, but meddle not with him.

LEIR.
> Friend, thy commission is to deal with me,
> And I am he that hath deserved all.
> The plot was laid to take away my life, 255
> And here it is; I do entreat thee take it.
> Yet for my sake and as thou art a man,
> Spare this my friend, that hither with me came.
> I brought him forth whereas he had not been 260
> But for good will to bear me company.
> He left his friends, his country, and his goods,
> And came with me in most extremity.
> Oh, if he should miscarry here and die,
> Who is the cause of it, but only I? 265

MESSENGER.
> Why, that am I; let that ne'er trouble thee.

LEIR.
> Oh no, 'tis I. Oh, had I now to give thee
> The monarchy of all the spacious world
> To save his life, I would bestow it on thee; 270
> But I have nothing but these tears and prayers

And the submission of a bended knee.

    Kneel.

Oh, if all this to mercy move thy mind,

Spare him; in heaven thou shalt like mercy find.

MESSENGER [*Aside*].

I am as hard to be moved as another; and yet,   275

methinks the strength of their persuasions

stirs me a little.

PERILLUS.

My friend, if fear of the almighty power

Have power to move thee, we have said enough.

But if thy mind be moveable with gold,   280

We have not presently to give it thee.

Yet to thyself thou mayst do greater good

To keep thy hands still undefiled from blood:

For do but well consider with thyself,

When thou hast finish'd this outrageous act   285

What horror still will haunt thee for the deed.

Think this again, that they which would incense

Thee for to be the butcher of their father,

When it is done, for fear it should be known,

Would make a means to rid thee from the world.   290

Oh, then art thou forever tied in chains

Of everlasting torments to endure,

Even in the hottest hole of grisly hell,

Such pains as never mortal tongue can tell.

It thunders. He quakes and lets fall the

dagger next to Perillus.

LEIR.

Oh, heavens be thanked; he will spare my friend; 295

Now, when thou wilt, come make an end of me.

He lets fall the other dagger.

PERILLUS.

Oh happy sight! He means to save my lord.

The King of Heaven continue this good mind.

LEIR.

Why stay'st thou to do execution?

MESSENGER.

I am as willful as you for your life; 300

I will not do it, now you do entreat me.

PERILLUS.

Ah, now I see thou hast some spark of grace.

MESSENGER.

Beshrew you for it; you have put it in me,

The parlousest old men that ere I heard.

Well, to be flat, I'll not meddle with you. 305

Here I found you, and here I'll leave you.

If any ask you why the case so stands,

Say that your tongues were better than your hands.

Exit Messenger.

PERILLUS.

> Farewell. If ever we together meet,
>
> It shall go hard but I will thee re-greet.-- 310
>
> Courage, my lord, the worst is overpast.
>
> Let us give thanks to God and hie us hence.

LEIR.

> Thou art deceived, for I am past the best
>
> And know not whither for to go from hence.
>
> Death had been better welcome unto me 315
>
> Than longer life to add more misery.

PERILLUS.

> It were not good to return from whence we came,
>
> Unto your daughter Ragan back again.
>
> Now let us go to France unto Cordella,
>
> Your youngest daughter; doubtless she will succour you. 320

LEIR.

> Oh, how can I persuade myself of that,
>
> Since the other two are quite devoid of love;
>
> To whom I was so kind, as that my gifts
>
> Might make them love me, if 'twere nothing else?

PERILLUS.

> No worldly gifts but grace from God on high 325
>
> Doth nourish virtue and true charity.
>
> Remember well what words Cordella spake
>
> What time you ask'd her how she lov'd your grace.

>   She said her love unto you was as much
>
>   As ought a child to bear unto her father.   330

LEIR.

>   But she did find my love was not to her
>
>   As should a father bear unto a child.

PERILLUS.

>   That makes not her love to be any less,
>
>   If she do love you as a child should do.
>
>   You have tried two; try one more for my sake.   335
>
>   I'll ne'er entreat you further trial make.
>
>   Remember well the dream you had of late,
>
>   And think what comfort it foretells to us.

LEIR.

>   Come truest friend that ever man possess'd;
>
>   I know thou counsel'st all things for the best.   340
>
>   If this third daughter play a kinder part,
>
>   It comes of God and not of my desert. *Exeunt.*

[Scene xx]

Enter the Gallian Ambassador solus.

AMBASSADOR.

>   There is, of late, news come unto the court
>
>   That old Lord Leir remains in Cambria.
>
>   I'll hie me thither presently to impart
>
>   My letters and my message unto him.
>
>   I never was less welcome to a place   5

> In all my lifetime than I have been hither,
> Especially unto the stately queen,
> Who would not cast one gracious look on me,
> But still with low'ring and suspicious eyes
> Would take exceptions at each word I spake; 10
> And fain she would have undermined me
> To know what my embassage did import.
> But she is like to hop without her hope,
> And in this matter for to want her will,
> Though by report she'll have't in all things else. 15
> Well, I will post away for Cambria;
> Within these few days, I hope to be there. *Exit.*

[Scene xxi]

> *Enter the King and Queen of Gallia and Mumford.*

KING.
> By this, our father understands our mind
> And our kind greetings sent to him of late;
> Therefore, my mind presageth, ere't be long,
> We shall receive from Britain happy news.

CORDELLA.
> I fear my sister will dissuade his mind, 5
> For she to me hath always been unkind.

KING.
> Fear not, my love; since that we know the worst,
> The last means helps, if that we miss the first.

155

>   If he'll not come to Gallia unto us,
>
>   Then we will sail to Britain unto him. 10

MUMFORD.
>   Well, if I once see Brittany again, I have
>   sworn I'll never come home without my wench;
>   and I'll not be forsworn. I'll rather never
>   come home while I live.

CORDELLA.
>   Are you sure, Mumford, she is a maid still? 15

MUMFORD.
>   Nay, I'll not swear she is a maid, but she goes
>   for one. I'll take her at all adventures, if I
>   can get her.

CORDELLA.
>   Aye, that's well put in.

MUMFORD.
>   Well put in? Nay, it was ill put in; for had it 20
>   been as well put in as ere I put in, in my days,
>   I would have made her follow me to France.

CORDELLA.
>   Nay, you'd have been so kind as take her with you;
>   or else, were I as she, I would have been so loving as I'd
>   stay behind you. Yet I must confess, you 25
>   are a very proper man and able to make a wench do
>   more than she would do.

MUMFORD.

>Well, I have a pair of slops for the nonce will hold all
>
>your mocks.

KING.

>Nay, we see you have a handsome hose.   30

CORDELLA.

>Aye, and of the newest fashion.

MUMFORD.

>More bobs, more; put them in still! They'll
>
>serve instead of bombast; yet put not in too
>
>many, lest the seams crack and they fly out
>
>amongst you again. You must not think to outface   35
>
>me so easily in my mistress' quarrel, who, if I
>
>see once again, ten team of horses shall not
>
>draw me away till I have full and whole possession.

KING.

>Aye, but one team and a cart will serve the turn.

CORDELLA.

>Not only for him but also for his wench.   40

MUMFORD.

>Well, you are two to one, I'll give you over.
>
>And since I see you so pleasantly disposed,
>
>Which indeed is but seldom seen, I'll claim
>
>A promise of you which you shall not deny me;
>
>for promise is debt, and by this hand, you

>promis'd it me. Therefore you owe it me, and
>you shall pay it me, or I'll sue you upon an
>action of unkindness.

KING.
>Prithee, Lord Mumford, what promise did I make thee?

MUMFORD.
>Faith, nothing but this: that the next fair   50
>weather, which is very now, you would go in
>progress down to the seaside, which is very
>near.

KING.
>Faith, in this motion I will join with thee
>And be a mediator to my queen.   55
>   [*To Cordella.*]
>Prithee, my love, let this match go forward;
>My mind foretells 'twill be a lucky voyage.

CORDELLA.
>Entreaty needs not where you may command.
>So you be pleas'd, I am right well content.
>Yet, as the sea I much desire to see,   60
>So am I most unwilling to be seen.

KING.
>We'll go disguised, all unknown to any.

CORDELLA.
>Howsoever you make one, I'll make another.

MUMFORD.
 And I the third. Oh, I am overjoyed!
 See what love is, which getteth with a word   65
 What all the world besides could ne'er obtain!
 But what disguises shall we have, my lord?

KING.
 Faith, thus: my queen and I will be disguis'd
 Like a plain country couple, and you shall be Roger,
 Our man, and wait upon us; or if you will,   70
 You shall go first and we will wait on you.

MUMFORD.
 'Twere more than time; this device is excellent.
 Come, let us about it. *Exeunt.*

[Scene xxii]

  Enter Cambria and Ragan with Nobles.

CAMBRIA.
 What strange mischance or unexpected hap
 Hath thus depriv'd us of our father's presence?
 Can no man tell us what's become of him,
 With whom we did converse not two days since?
 My lords, let everywhere light-horse be sent   5
 To scour about through all our regiment.
 Dispatch a post immediately to Cornwall
 To see if any news be of him there.
 Myself will make a strict inquiry here

      And all about our cities near at hand,   10

      Till certain news of his abode be brought.

RAGAN.

      All sorrow is but counterfeit to mine,

      Whose lips are almost sealed up with grief.

      Mine is the substance whilst they do but seem

      To weep the loss which tears cannot redeem.   15

      Oh, ne'er was heard so strange a misadventure,

      A thing so far beyond the reach of sense,

      Since no man's reason in the cause can enter.

      What hath remov'd my father thus from hence?

      Oh, I do fear some charm or invocation   20

      Of wicked spirits or infernal fiends,

      Stirr'd by Cordella, moves this innovation

      And brings my father timeless to his end.

      But might I know that the detested witch

      Were certain cause of this uncertain ill,   25

      Myself to France would go in some disguise

      And with these nails scratch out her hateful eyes;

      For since I am deprived of my father,

      I loathe my life and wish my death the rather.

CAMBRIA.

      The heavens are just and hate impiety,   30

      And will, no doubt, reveal such heinous crimes;

      Censure not any till you know the right.

  Let him be judge that bringeth truth to light.

RAGAN.
  Oh, but my grief, like to a swelling tide,
  Exceeds the bounds of common patience; 35
  Nor can I moderate my tongue so much
  To conceal them whom I hold in suspect.

CAMBRIA.
  This matter shall be sifted; if it be she,
  A thousand Frances shall not harbor her.

Enter the Gallian Ambassador.

AMBASSADOR.
  All happiness unto the Cambrian king. 40

CAMBRIA.
  Welcome, my friend; from whence is thy embassage?

AMBASSADOR.
  I came from Gallia unto Cornwall, sent
  With letters to your honorable father,
  Whom there not finding, as I did expect,
  I was directed hither to repair. 45

RAGAN.
  Frenchman, what is thy message to my father?

AMBASSADOR.
  My letters, madam, will import the same,
  Which my commission is for to deliver.

RAGAN.

    In his absence you may trust us with your letters.

AMBASSADOR.

    I must perform my charge in such a manner   50

    As I have strict commandment from the king.

RAGAN.

    There is good packing 'twixt your king and you.

    You need not hither come to ask for him;

    You know where he is better than ourselves.

AMBASSADOR.

    Madam, I hope not far off.   55

RAGAN.

    Hath the young murd'ress, your outrageous queen,

    No means to color her detested deeds

    In finishing my guiltless father's days

    Because he gave her nothing to her dower,

    But by the color of a fain'd embassage   60

    To send him letters hither to our court?

    Go, carry them to them that sent them hither,

    And bid them keep their scrolls unto themselves;

    They cannot blind us with such slight excuse

    To smother up so monstrous vile abuse.   65

    And were it not--it is--'gainst law of arms

    To offer violence to a messenger,

    We would inflict such torments on thyself

As should enforce thee to reveal the truth.

AMBASSADOR.

Madam, your threats no whit appall my mind; 70

I know my conscience guiltless of this act.

My king and queen, I dare be sworn, are free

From any thought of such impiety.

And therefore, madam, you have done them wrong,

And ill-beseeming with a sister's love, 75

Who in mere duty tender him as much

As ever you respected him for dower.

The king, your husband, will not say as much.

CAMBRIA.

I will suspend my judgment for a time

Till more appearance give us further light; 80

Yet, to be plain, your coming doth enforce

A great suspicion to our doubtful mind,

And that you do resemble, to be brief,

Him that first robs and then cries, "Stop the thief."

AMBASSADOR.

Pray God some near you have not done the like. 85

RAGAN.

Hence, saucy mate, reply no more to us;

She strikes him.

For law of arms shall not protect thy tongue.

AMBASSADOR.

    Ne'er was I offer'd such discourtesy.

    God and my king, I trust, ere it be long

    Will find a mean to remedy this wrong.   90

Exit Ambassador.

RAGAN.

    How shall I live to suffer this disgrace

    At every base and vulgar peasant's hands?

    It ill befitteth my imperial state

    To be thus used, and no man take my part.

    She weeps.

CAMBRIA.

    What should I do? Infringe the law of arms   95

    Were to my everlasting obloquy;

    But I will take revenge upon his master

    Which sent him hither to delude us thus.

RAGAN.

    Nay, if you put up this, be sure ere long,

    Now that my father thus is made away,   100

    She'll come and claim a third part of your crown

    As due unto her by inheritance.

CAMBRIA.

    But I will prove her title to be nought

    But shame and the reward of parricide,

    And make her an example to the world   105

> For after-ages to admire her penance.
>
> This will I do as I am Cambria's king,
>
> Or lose my life to prosecute revenge.
>
> Come, first let's learn what news is of our father,
>
> And then proceed as best occasion fits. *Exeunt.* 110

[Scene xxiii]

Enter Leir and Perillus, and two mariners in sea-gowns and sea-caps.

PERILLUS.
> My honest friends, we are asham'd to show
>
> The great extremity of our present state,
>
> In that at this time we are brought so low
>
> That we want money for to pay our passage.
>
> The truth is so: we met with some good fellows 5
>
> A little before we came aboard your ship
>
> Which stripp'd us quite of all the coin we had
>
> And left us not a penny in our purses.
>
> Yet wanting money, we will use the mean
>
> To see you satisfied to the uttermost. 10

FIRST MARINER (*Look on Leir*).
> Here's a good gown; 'twould become me passing well;
>
> I should be fine in it.

SECOND MARINER (*Look on Perillus*).
> Here's a good cloak; I marvel how I should look in it.

LEIR.

>Faith, had we others to supply their room,
>
>Though ne'er so mean, you willingly should have them.   15

FIRST MARINER.

>Do you hear, sir? You look like an honest man.
>I'll not stand to do you a pleasure. Here's a
>good strong motley gaberdine, cost me fourteen
>good shillings at Billingsgate; give me your
>gown for it and your cap for mine, and I'll for-   20
>give your passage.

LEIR.

>With all my heart and twenty thanks.
>
>>*Leir and he changeth.*

SECOND MARINER [*To Perillus*].

>Do you hear, sir? You shall have a better match
>than he, because you are my friend. Here is a
>good sheep's russet seagown will bide more stress,   25
>I warrant you, than two of his. Yet, for you seem
>to be an honest gentleman, I am content to change
>it for your cloak and ask you nothing for your
>passage more.
>
>>*Pull off Perillus' cloak.*

PERILLUS.

>My own I willingly would change with thee
>And think myself indebted to thy kindness,

But would my friend might keep his garment still. 30
My friend, I'll give thee this new doublet if thou wilt
Restore his gown unto him back again.

FIRST MARINER.

Nay, if I do, would I might ne'er eat powder'd beef
and mustard more, nor drink can of good liquor whilst
I live. My friend, you have small reason to seek to 35
hinder me of my bargain; but the best is, a bargain's
a bargain.

LEIR. *(To Perillus)*.

Kind friend, it is much better as it is;
For by this means we may escape unknown
Till time and opportunity do fit. 40

SECOND MARINER.

Hark, hark, they are laying their heads together;
they'll repent them of their bargain anon. 'Twere
best for us to go while we are well.

FIRST MARINER.

God be with you, sir; for your passage back again,
I'll use you as unreasonable as another. 45

LEIR.

I know thou wilt, but we hope to bring ready
money with us when we come back again.--*Exeunt Mariners*.
Were ever men in this extremity,
In a strange country, and devoid of friends,

And not a penny for to help ourselves?

Kind friend, what think'st thou will become of us? 50

PERILLUS.

Be of good cheer, my lord; I have a doublet

Will yield us money enough to serve our turns

Until we come unto your daughter's court.

And then I hope, we shall find friends enough.

LEIR.

Ah, kind Perillus, that is it I fear, 55

And makes me faint or ever I come there

Can kindness spring out of ingratitude?

Or love be reap'd where hatred hath been sown?

Can henbane join in league with mithridate?

Or sugar grow in wormwood's bitter stalk? 60

It cannot be; they are too opposite,

And so am I to any kindness here

I have thrown wormwood on the sugar'd youth,

And like to henbane poisoned the fount

Whence flowed the mithridate of a child's good will. 65

I, like an envious thorn, have prick'd the heart

And turn'd sweet grapes to sour unrelish'd sloes.

The causeless ire of my respectless breast

Hath sour'd the sweet milk of Dame Nature's paps.

My bitter words have gall'd her honey thoughts, 70

And weeds of rancor chok'd the flower of grace.

Then what remainder is of any hope,

But all our fortunes will go quite aslope?

PERILLUS.

Fear not, my lord, the perfect good indeed

Can never be corrupted by the bad. 75

A new fresh vessel still retains the taste

Of that which first is pour'd into the same.

And therefore, though you name yourself the thorn,

The weed, the gall, the henbane, and the wormwood,

Yet she'll continue in her former state, 80

The honey, milk, grape, sugar, mithridate.

LEIR.

Thou pleasing orator unto me in woe,

Cease to beguile me with thy hopeful speeches.

Oh, join with me and think of nought but crosses,

And then we'll one lament another's losses. 85

PERILLUS.

Why, say the worst. The worst can be but death,

And death is better than for to despair.

Then hazard death which may convert to life;

Banish despair which brings a thousand deaths.

LEIR.

O'ercome with thy strong arguments, I yield 90

To be directed by thee as thou wilt.

As thou yield'st comfort to my crazed thoughts,

Would I could yield the like unto thy body

Which is full weak. I know, and ill apaid,

For want of fresh meat and due sustenance. 95

PERILLUS.

Alack, my lord, my heart doth bleed to think

That you should be in such extremity.

LEIR.

Come, let us go and see what God will send;

When all means fail, He is the surest friend. *Exeunt.*

[Scene xxiv]

Enter the Gallian King and Queen and Mumford
with a basket, disguised like country folk.

KING.

This tedious journey all on foot, sweet love,

Cannot be pleasing to your tender joints

Which ne'er were used to these toilsome walks.

CORDELLA.

I never in my life took more delight

In any journey than I do in this; 5

It did me good, whenas we happ'd to light

Amongst the merry crew of country folk,

To see what industry and pains they took

To win them commendations 'mongst their friends.

Lord, how they labor to bestir themselves, 10

And in their quirks to go beyond the moon,

>   And so take on them with such antic fits
>
>   That one would think they were beside their wits!
>
>   Come away, Roger, with your basket.

MUMFORD.

>   Soft, dame, here comes a couple of old youths.   15
>
>   I must needs make myself fat with jesting at them.
>
>   *Enter Leir and Perillus very faintly.*

CORDELLA.

>   Nay, prithee do not; they do seem to be
>
>   Men much o'ergone with grief and misery.
>
>   Let's stand aside and harken what they say.

LEIR.

>   Ah, my Perillus, now I see we both   20
>
>   Shall end our days in this unfruitful soil.
>
>   Oh, I do faint for want of sustenance,
>
>   And thou, I know, in little better case.
>
>   No gentle tree affords one taste of fruit
>
>   To comfort us until we meet with men.   25
>
>   No lucky path conducts our luckless steps
>
>   Unto a place where any comfort dwells.
>
>   Sweet rest betide unto our happy souls,
>
>   For here I see our bodies must have end.

PERILLUS.

>   Ah, my dear lord, how doth my heart lament   30
>
>   To see you brought to this extremity!

Oh, if you love me as you do profess,

Or ever thought well of me in my life,

He strips up his arms.

Feed on this flesh, whose veins are not so dry

But there is virtue left to comfort you. 35

Oh, feed on this; if this will do you good,

I'll smile for joy to see you suck my blood.

LEIR.

I am no cann'bal that I should delight

To slake my hungry jaws with human flesh.

I am no devil or ten times worse than so 40

To suck the blood of such a peerless friend.

Oh, do not think that I respect my life

So dearly as I do thy loyal love.

Ah, Brittayne, I shall never see thee more,

That hast unkindly banished thy king. 45

And yet not thou dost make me to complain,

But they which were more near to me than thou.

CORDELLA [*Aside*].

What do I hear? This lamentable voice

Methinks, ere now, I oftentimes have heard.

LEIR.

Ah, Gonorill, was half my kingdom's gift 50

The cause that thou didst seek to have my life?

Ah, cruel Ragan, did I give thee all,

> And all could not suffice without my blood?
> Ah, poor Cordella, did I give thee nought?
> Nor never shall be able for to give? 55
> Oh, let me warn all ages that ensueth
> How they trust flattery and reject the truth.
> Well, unkind girls, I here forgive you both
> (Yet the just heavens will hardly do the like)
> And only crave forgiveness at the end 60
> Of good Cordella, and of thee, my friend;
> Of God, whose majesty I have offended
> By my transgression many thousand ways;
> Of her, dear heart, whom I for no occasion
> Turn'd out of all through flatterers' persuasion; 65
> Of thee, kind friend, who but for me, I know,
> Had'st never come unto this place of woe.

CORDELLA.
> Alack, that ever I should live to see
> My noble father in this misery.

KING.
> Sweet love, reveal not what thou art as yet, 70
> Until we know the ground of all this ill.

CORDELLA.
> Oh, but some meat, some meat! Do you not see
> How near they are to death for want of food?
>
> *[A table with food and drink is brought forward.]*

PERILLUS.

    Lord, which did'st help thy servants at their need,

    Or now or never send us help with speed.   75

    Oh comfort, comfort! Yonder is a banquet

    And men and women, my lord; be of good cheer,

    For I see comfort coming very near.

    Oh, my lord, a banquet, and men and women!

LEIR.

    Oh, let kind pity mollify their hearts   80

    That they may help us in our great extremes.

PERILLUS.

    God save you friends, and if this blessed banquet

    Affordeth any food or sustenance,

    Even for His sake that saved us all from death,

    Vouchsafe to save us from the grip of famine.   85

CORDELLA. (*She bringeth him to the table*).

    Here, father, sit and eat; here, sit and drink

    And would it were far better for your sakes.

        Perillus takes Leir by the hand to the table.

PERILLUS.

    I'll give you thanks anon; my friend doth faint

    And needeth present comfort.

        Leir drinks.

MUMFORD.

    I warrant he ne'er stays to say grace.   90

Oh, there's no sauce to a good stomach.

PERILLUS.

The blessed God of Heaven hath thought upon us.

LEIR.

The thanks be His and these kind courteous folk,

By whose humanity we are preserved.

They eat hungrily; Leir drinks.

CORDELLA.

And may that draft be unto him as was 95

That which old Aeson drank, which did renew

His withered age and made him young again.

And may that meat be unto him as was

That which Elias ate, in strength whereof

He walked forty days and never fainted. 100

Shall I conceal me longer from my father,

Or shall I manifest myself to him?

KING.

Forbear awhile until his strength return

Lest, being overjoyed with seeing thee,

His poor weak senses should forsake their office 105

And so our cause of joy be turn'd to sorrow.

PERILLUS.

What cheer, my lord? How do you feel yourself?

LEIR.

Methinks I never ate such savory meat.

> It is as pleasant as the blessed manna
>
> That rain'd from heaven amongst the Israelites. 110
>
> It hath recall'd my spirits home again
>
> And made me fresh as erst I was before.
>
> But how shall we congratulate their kindness?

PERILLUS.

> In faith, I know not how sufficiently,
>
> But the best mean that I can think on is this: 115
>
> I'll offer them my doublet in requital,
>
> For we have nothing else to spare.

LEIR.

> Nay, stay, Perillus, for they shall have mine.

PERILLUS.

> Pardon, my lord; I swear they shall have mine.
>
> *Perillus proffers his doublet; they will not take it.*

LEIR.

> Ah, who would think such kindness should remain 120
>
> Among such strange and unacquainted men,
>
> And that such hate should harbor in the breast
>
> Of those which have occasion to be best?

CORDELLA.

> Ah, good old father, tell to me thy grief.
>
> I'll sorrow with thee, if not add relief. 125

LEIR.

> Ah, good young daughter; I may call thee so,

>For thou art like a daughter I did owe.

CORDELLA.
>Do you not owe her still? What, is she dead?

LEIR.
>No, God forbid; but all my interest's gone,
>By showing myself too much unnatural. 130
>So have I lost the title of a father,
>And may be call'd a stranger to her rather.

CORDELLA.
>Your title's good still, for 'tis always known
>A man may do as him list with his own.
>But have you but one daughter then in all? 135

LEIR.
>Yes, I have more by two than would I had.

CORDELLA.
>Oh, say not so, but rather see the end:
>They that are bad may have the grace to mend.
>But how have they offended you so much?

LEIR.
>If from the first I should relate the cause, 140
>'Twould make a heart of adamant to weep;
>And thou, poor soul, kindhearted as thou art,
>Dost weep already ere I do begin.

CORDELLA.
>   For God's love, tell it; and when you have done,
>   I'll tell the reason why I weep so soon. 145

LEIR.
>   Then know this first: I am a Briton born
>   And had three daughters by one loving wife;
>   And, though I say it, of beauty they were sped,
>   Especially the youngest of the three,
>   For her perfections hardly match'd could be. 150
>   On these I doted with a jealous love,
>   And thought to try which of them lov'd me best
>   By asking them which would do most for me.
>   The first and second flatter'd me with words
>   And vow'd they lov'd me better than their lives. 155
>   The youngest said she loved me as a child
>   Might do; her answer I esteem'd most vild,
>   And presently in an outrageous mood
>   I turn'd her from me to go sink or swim;
>   And all I had, even to the very clothes, 160
>   I gave in dowry with the other two;
>   And she that best deserv'd the greatest share,
>   I gave her nothing but disgrace and care.
>   Now mark the sequel. When I had done thus,
>   I sojourn'd in my eldest daughter's house 165

Where, for a time, I was entreated well,

And liv'd in state sufficing my content.

But every day her kindness did grow cold,

Which I, with patience, put up well enough,

And seemed not to see the things I saw; 170

But at the last, she grew so far incens'd

With moody fury and with causeless hate

That in most vile and contumelious terms

She bade me pack and harbor somewhere else.

Then was I fain, for refuge, to repair 175

Unto my other daughter for relief,

Who gave me pleasing and most courteous words,

But in her actions showed herself so sore

As never any daughter did before.

She pray'd me in a morning out betime 180

To go to a thicket two miles from the court,

'Pointing that there she would come talk with me.

There she had set a shag-hair'd murd'ring wretch

To massacre my honest friend and me.

Then judge yourself, although my tale be brief, 185

If ever man had greater cause of grief.

KING.

Nor never like impiety was done

Since the creation of the world begun.

LEIR.
> And now I am constrain'd to seek relief
> Of her to whom I have been so unkind,   190
> Whose censure, if it do award me death,
> I must confess she pays me but my due.
> But if she show a loving daughter's part,
> It comes of God and her, not my desert.

CORDELLA.
> No doubt she will; I dare be sworn she will.   195

LEIR.
> How know you that, not knowing what she is?

CORDELLA.
> Myself a father have a great way hence,
> Us'd me as ill as ever you did her;
> Yet, that his reverend age I once might see,
> I'd creep along to meet him on my knee.   200

LEIR.
> Oh, no men's children are unkind but mine.

CORDELLA.
> Condemn not all because of others' crime.
> But look, dear father; look, behold, and see
> Thy loving daughter speaketh unto thee.
>   *She kneels.*

LEIR.
> Oh, stand thou up; it is my part to kneel   205

And ask forgiveness for my former faults.

> *He kneels.*

CORDELLA.

Oh, if you wish I should enjoy my breath

Dear father rise, or I receive my death.

> *He riseth.*

LEIR.

Then I will rise to satisfy you mind,

But kneel again 'til pardon be resign'd.   210

> *He kneels.*

CORDELLA.

I pardon you; the word beseems not me,

But I do say so for to ease your knee.

You gave me life; you were the cause that I

Am what I am, who else had never been.

LEIR.

But you gave life to me and to my friend,   215

Whose days had else had an untimely end.

CORDELLA.

You brought me up whenas I was but young

And far unable for to help myself.

LEIR.

I cast thee forth whenas thou wast but young

And far unable for to help thyself.   220

CORDELLA.
>God, world, and nature say I do you wrong,
>
>That can endure to see you kneel so long.

KING.
>Let me break off this loving controversy,
>
>Which doth rejoice my very soul to see.
>
>Good father, rise; she is your loving daughter.   225
>
>>*He riseth.*
>
>And honors you with as respective duty
>
>As if you were the monarch of the world.

CORDELLA.
>But I will never rise from off my knee,
>
>>*She kneels.*
>
>Until I have your blessing and your pardon
>
>Of all my faults committed any way   230
>
>From my first birth unto this present day.

LEIR.
>The blessing which the God of Abraham gave
>
>Unto the tribe of Judah light on thee
>
>And multiply thy days, that thou mayst see
>
>They children's children prosper after thee.   235
>
>Thy faults, which are just none that I do know,
>
>God pardon on high and I forgive below.
>
>>*She riseth.*

CORDELLA.
>Now is my heart at quiet and doth leap
>Within my breast for joy of this good hap;
>And now, dear father, welcome to our court, 240
>And welcome, kind Perillus, unto me,
>Mirror of virtue and true honesty.

LEIR.
>Oh, he hath been the kindest friend to me
>That ever man had in adversity.

PERILLUS.
>My tongue doth fail to say what heart doth think,
>I am so ravish'd with exceeding joy.

KING.
>All you have spoke; now let me speak my mind,
>And in few words much matter here conclude.
>   *He kneels.*
>If ere my heart do harbor any joy,
>Or true content repose within my breast, 250
>Till I have rooted out this viperous sect
>And repossess'd my father of his crown,
>Let me be counted for the perjur'dst man
>That ever spake word since the world began.
>   *Rise.*

MUMFORD.
>Let me pray too, that never pray'd before. 255

> *Mumford kneels.*
>
> If ere I resalute the British earth,
>
> As ere't be long I do presume I shall,
>
> And do return from thence without my wench,
>
> Let me be gelded for my recompense.
>
> > *Rise.*

KING.
> Come, let's to arms for to redress this wrong; 260
>
> Till I am there, methinks the time seems long. *Exeunt.*

[Scene xxv]

> *Enter Ragan sola.*

RAGAN.
> I feel a hell of conscience in my breast,
>
> Tormenting me with horror for my fact
>
> And makes me in an agony of doubt,
>
> For fear the world should find my dealing out.
>
> The slave whom I appointed for the act, 5
>
> I ne'er set eye upon the peasant since.
>
> Oh, could I get him for to make him sure,
>
> My doubts would cease and I should rest secure;
>
> But if the old men with persuasive words
>
> Have sav'd their lives and made him to relent, 10
>
> Then are they fled unto the court of France
>
> And like a trumpet manifest my shame.
>
> A shame on these white-liver'd slaves, say I,

That with fair words so soon are overcome.
Oh, God, that I had been but made a man, 15
Or that my strength were equal with my will!
These foolish men are nothing but mere pity,
And melt as butter doth against the sun.
Why should they have preeminence over us,
Since we are creatures of more brave resolve? 20
I swear I am quite out of charity
With all the heartless men in Christendom.
A pox upon them when they are afraid
To give a stab or slit a paltry windpipe,
Which are so easy matters to be done. 25
Well, had I thought the slave would serve me so,
Myself would have been executioner.
'Tis now undone, and if that it be know,
I'll make as good shift as I can for one.
He that repines at me, howe'er it stands, 30
'Twere best for him to keep him from my hands. *Exit.*

[Scene xxvi]

Sound drums and trumpets. Enter the Gallian King,

Leir, Mumford and the army.

KING.

Thus have we brought our army to the sea,
Whereas our ships are ready to receive us.
The wind stands fair, and we in four hours' sail

May easily arrive on British shore

Where, unexpected, we may them surprise 5

And gain a glorious victory with ease.

Wherefore, my loving countrymen, resolve,

Since truth and justice fighteth on our sides,

That we shall march with conquest where we go.

Myself will be as forward as the first, 10

And step by step march with the hardiest wight,

And not the meanest soldier in our camp

Shall be in danger but I'll second him.

To you, my lord, we give the whole command

Of all the army, next unto ourself, 15

Not doubting of you; but you will extend

Your wonted valor in this needful case,

Encouraging the rest to do the like

By your approved magnanimity.

MUMFORD.

My liege, 'tis needless to spur a willing horse 20

That's apt enough to run himself to death;

For here I swear by that sweet saint's bright eyes,

Which are the stars which guide me to good hap,

Either to see my old lord crown'd anew,

Or in his cause to bid the world adieu. 25

LEIR.

Thanks, good Lord Mumford; 'tis more of your good will

>   Than any merit or desert in me.

MUMFORD.
>   And now to you, my worthy countrymen,
>   Ye valiant race of Genovestan Gauls,
>   Surnamed Redshanks for your chivalry,   30
>   Because you fight up to the shanks in blood,
>   Show yourselves now to be right Gauls indeed
>   And be so bitter on your enemies
>   That they may say you are as bitter as gall.
>   Gall them, brave shot, with your artillery!   35
>   Gall them, brave halberds, with your sharp-point bills,
>   Each in their 'pointed place; not one, but all
>   Fight for the credit of yourselves and Gaul.

KING.
>   Then what should more persuasion need to those
>   That rather wish to deal than hear of blows?   40
>   Let's to our ships, and, if that God permit,
>   In four hours' sail I hope we shall be there.

MUMFORD.
>   And in five hours more, I make no doubt,
>   But we shall bring our wish'd desires about. *Exeunt.*

[Scene xxvii]

>   *Enter a captain of the watch and two watchmen.*

CAPTAIN.
>   My honest friends, it is your turn tonight

> To watch in this place near about the beacon.
>
> And vigilantly have regard
>
> If any fleet of ships pass hitherward;
>
> Which if you do, your office is to fire 5
>
> The beacon presently and raise the town. *Exit.*

FIRST WATCHMAN.

> Aye, aye, aye, fear nothing; we know our charge,
>
> I warrant I have been a watchman about this beacon
>
> this thirty year, and yet I ne'er see it stir but
>
> stood as quietly as might be. 10

SECOND WATCHMAN.

> Faith, neighbor, and you'll follow my 'vice,
>
> instead of watching the beacon, we'll go to goodman
>
> Jennings and watch a pot of ale and a rasher of ba-
>
> con; and if we do not drink ourselves drunk, then
>
> so; I warrant, the beacon will see us when we come 15
>
> out again.

FIRST WATCHMAN.

> Aye, but how if somebody excuse us to the captain?

SECOND WATCHMAN.

> 'Tis no matter; I'll prove by good reason that we
>
> watch the beacon, ass for example--

FIRST WATCHMAN.

> I hope you do not call me ass by craft, neighbor. 20

SECOND WATCHMAN.

> No, no, but for example; say here stands the pot of ale, that's the beacon.

FIRST WATCHMAN.

> Aye, aye, 'tis a very good beacon.

SECOND WATCHMAN.

> Well, say here stands your nose; that's the fire.

FIRST WATCHMAN.

> Indeed, I must confess 'tis somewhat red. 25

SECOND WATCHMAN.

> I see come marching in a dish half a score pieces of salt bacon.

FIRST WATCHMAN.

> I understand your meaning; that's as much to say, half a score ships.

SECOND WATCHMAN.

> True, you conster right; presently, like 30
> a faithful watchman, I fire the beacon and call up the town.

FIRST WATCHMAN.

> Aye, that's as much as to say you set your nose to the pot and drink up the drink.

SECOND WATCHMAN.

> You are in the right; come, let's go fire the 35
> beacon. *Exeunt.*

[Scene xxvii]

Enter the King of Gallia with a still march,

Mumford and soldiers.

KING.

Now march our ensigns on the British earth,

And we are near approaching to the town;

Then look about you, valiant countrymen,

And we shall finish this exploit with ease.

Th'inhabitants of this mistrustful place 5

Are dead asleep, as men that are secure.

Here shall we skirmish but with naked men,

Devoid of sense, new waked from a dream,

That know not what our coming doth pretend,

Till they do feel our meaning on their skins. 10

Therefore, assail! God and our right for us! *Exeunt.*

[Scene xxix]

Alarum, with men and women half naked. Enter

two captains without doublets, with swords.

FIRST CAPTAIN.

Where are these villains that were set to watch

And fire the beacon if occasion serv'd,

That thus have suffer'd us to be surpris'd

And never given notice to the town?

We are betray'd and quite devoid of hope 5

By any means to fortify ourselves.

SECOND CAPTAIN.

    'Tis ten to one the peasants are o'ercome

    with drink and sleep, and so neglect their charge.

FIRST CAPTAIN.

    A whirlwind carry them quick to a whirlpool,

    That there the slaves may drink their bellies full.   10

SECOND CAPTAIN.

    This 'tis, to have the beacon so near the ale house.

        Enter the watchmen drunk, with each a pot.

FIRST CAPTAIN.

    Out on ye, villains; whither run you now?

FIRST WATCHMAN.

    To fire the town and call up the beacon!

SECOND WATCHMAN.

    No, no sir, to fire the beacon.

        He drinks.

SECOND CAPTAIN.

    What? With a pot of ale, you drunken rogues?   15

FIRST CAPTAIN.

    You'll fire the beacon when the town is lost!

    I'll teach you how to tend your office better.

        Draw to stab them.

        Enter Mumford; Captains run away.

MUMFORD.

    Yield, yield, yield!

He kicks down their pots.

FIRST WATCHMAN.

    Reel? No, we do not reel. You may

    lack a pot of ale ere you die.   20

MUMFORD.

    But in meanspace, I answer, you want none.

    Well, there's no dealing with you; y'are tall

    men and well weaponed. I would there were no

    worse than you in the town. *Exit.*

SECOND WATCHMAN.

    'A speaks like an honest man; my choler's past   25

    already. Come neighbor, let's go.

FIRST WATCHMAN.

    Nay, first let's see and we can stand. *Exeunt.*

    Alarum, excursions, Mumford after them and some half

    naked. Enter the Gallian king, Leir, Mumford, Cordella,

    Perillus, and soldiers with the chief of the town bound.

KING.

    Fear not, my friends; you shall receive no hurt

    If you'll subscribe unto your lawful king,

    And quite revoke your fealty from Cambria   30

    And from aspiring Cornwall too, whose wives

    Have practic'd treason 'gainst their father's life.

    We come in justice of your wronged king

    And do intend no harm at all to you,

    So you submit unto your lawful king. 35

LEIR.
    Kind countrymen, it grieves me that perforce
    I am constrain'd to use extremities.

NOBLEMAN.
    Long have you here been look'd for, good my lord,
    And wish'd for by a general consent;
    And had we known your highness had arrived, 40
    We had not made resistance to your grace.
    And now, my gracious lord, you need not doubt
    But all the country will yield presently,
    Which, since your absence, have been greatly tax'd
    For to maintain their overswelling pride. 45
    We'll presently send word to all our friends;
    When they have notice, they will come apace.

LEIR.
    Thanks, loving subjects, and thanks, worthy son;
    Thanks, my kind daughter; thanks to you, my lord,
    Who willingly adventured have your blood 50
    Without desert to do me so much good.

MUMFORD.
    Oh, say not so;
    I have been much beholding to your grace.
    I must confess I have been in some skirmishes,
    But I was never in the like to this; 55

> For where I was wont to meet with armed men,
>
> I was now encounter'd with naked women.

CORDELLA.

> We that are feeble and want use of arms
>
> Will pray to God to shield you from all harms.

LEIR.

> The while your hands do manage ceaseless toil, 60
>
> Our hearts shall pray the foes may have the foil.

PERILLUS.

> We'll fast and pray whilst you for us do fight,
>
> That victory may prosecute the right.

KING.

> Methinks your words do amplify, my friends,
>
> And add fresh vigor to my willing limbs. 65

Drum [sounds].

> But hark, I hear the adverse drum approach.
>
> God and our right, Saint Denis and Saint George!

Enter Cornwall, Cambria, Gonorill, Ragan

and the Army.

CORNWALL.

> Presumptuous King of Gauls, how darest thou
>
> Presume to enter on our British shore?
>
> And more than that, to take our towns perforce 70
>
> And draw our subjects' hearts from their true king?
>
> Be sure to buy it at as dear a price

As e'er you bought presumption in your lives.

KING.

O'erdaring Cornwall, know we came in right
And just revengement of the wronged king, 75
Whose daughters there, fell vipers as they are,
Have sought to murder and deprive of life;
But God protected him from all their spite,
And we are come in justice of his right.

CAMBRIA.

Nor he nor thou have any interest here 80
But what you win and purchase with the sword.
Thy slanders to our noble virtuous queens
We'll in the battle thrust them down thy throat
Except, for fear of our revenging hands,
Thou fly to sea as not secure on lands. 85

MUMFORD.

Welshman, I'll so ferret you ere night for that
word that you shall have no mind to crake so well
this twelvemonth.

GONORILL.

They lie that say we sought our father's death.

RAGAN.

'Tis merely forged for a color's sake 90
To set a gloss on your invasion.
Methinks an old man ready for to die

Should be asham'd to broach so foul a lie.

CORDELLA.

    Fie, shameless sister, so devoid of grace

    To call our father liar to his face.   95

GONORILL.

    Peace, puritan, dissembling hypocrite,

    Which art so good that thou wilt prove stark naught.

    Anon, whenas I have you in my fingers,

    I'll make you wish yourself in purgatory.

PERILLUS.

    Nay, peace, thou monster, shame unto thy sex,   100

    Thou fiend in likeness of a human creature.

RAGAN.

    I never heard a fouler spoken man.

LEIR.

    Out on thee, viper, scum, filthy parricide,

    More odious to my sight than is a toad;

    Knowest thou these letters?   105

        She snatches them and tears them.

RAGAN.

    Think you to outface me with your paltry scrolls?

    You come to drive my husband from his right

    Under the color of a forged letter.

LEIR.

    Whoever heard the like impiety?

PERILLUS.

>You are our debtor of more patience;   110
>
>We were more patient when we stay'd for you
>
>Within the thicket two long hours and more

RAGAN.

>What hours? What thicket?

PERILLUS.

>There where you sent your servant with your letters,
>
>Seal'd with your hand, to send us both to heaven,   115
>
>Where, as I think, you never mean to come.

RAGAN.

>Alas, you are grown a child again with age,
>
>Or else your senses dote for want of sleep.

PERILLUS.

>Indeed you made us rise betimes, you know,
>
>Yet had a care we should sleep where you bade us stay,   120
>
>But never wake more till the latter day.

GONORILL.

>Peace, peace, old fellow; thou are sleepy still.

MUMFORD.

>Faith, and if you reason till tomorrow,
>
>You get no other answer at their hands.
>
>'Tis pity two such good faces   125
>
>Should have so little grace between them.
>
>Well, let us see if their husbands with their hands

Can do as much as they do with their tongues.

CAMBRIA.

Aye, with their swords they'll make your tongue unsay

What they have said, or else they'll cut them out. 130

KING.

To't, gallants, to't, let's not stand brawling thus.

Exeunt both armies.

Sound alarum; excursions. Mumford must chase

Cambria away, then cease. Enter Cornwall.

CORNWALL.

The day is lost; our friends do all revolt

And join against us with the adverse part.

Ther is no means of safety but by flight,

And therefore I'll to Cornwall with my queen. *Exit.* 135

Enter Cambria.

CAMBRIA.

I think there is a devil in the camp hath haunted

me today; he hath so tired me that in a manner I

can fight no more.

Enter Mumford.

Zounds! Here he comes; I'll take me to my horse. *Exit.*

Mumford follows him to the door and returns.

MUMFORD.

Farewell, Welshman, give thee but thy due; 140

Thou hast a light and nimble pair of legs.

Thou art more in debt to them than to thy hands.

But if I meet thee once again today,

I'll cut them off and set them to a better heart. *Exit.*

Alarums and excursions, then sound victory.

Enter Leir, Perillus, King, Cordella, and Mumford.

KING.

Thanks be to God, your foes are overcome 145

And you again possessed of your right.

LEIR.

First to the heavens, next thanks to you, my son,

By whose good means I repossess the same;

Which if it please you to accept yourself,

With all my heart I will resign to you 150

For it is yours by right, and none of mine.

First have you rais'd at your own charge a power

Of valiant soldiers; this comes all from you.

Next have you ventured you own person's scathe;

And lastly, worthy Gallia never stain'd, 155

My kingly title I by thee have gain'd.

KING.

Thank heavens, not me; my zeal to you is such,

Command my utmost, I will never grutch.

CORDELLA.

He that with all kind love entreats his queen

Will not be to her father unkind seen. 160

LEIR.
> Ah, my Cordella, now I call to mind
> The modest answer which I took unkind,
> But now I see I am no whit beguil'd;
> Thou lovedst me dearly, and as ought a child.
> And thou, Perillus, partner once in woe, 165
> Thee to requite, the best I can, I'll do;
> Yet all I can, aye, were it ne'er so much.
> Were not sufficient, thy true lover is such.
> Thanks, worthy Mumford, to thee last of all,
> Not greeted last 'cause thy desert was small; 170
> No, thou hast lion-like laid on today.
> Chasing the Cornwall king and Cambria,
> Who with my daughters (daughters did I say?),
> To save their lives, the fugitives did play.
> Come, son and daughter, who did me advance; 175
> Repose with me awhile, and then for France.
>
> *Sound drums and trumpets. Exeunt.*
> FINIS

ENDNOTES

[Scene i]

    0.3 ACTUS I] Except for this one designation, there are no act or scene divisions in Q.

    0.4 Scene i] MSR; *Scene I, Presence chamber in King Leir's palace at Troynovant* Lee; *Erste Szene, Leir's Schloss* Fischer.

    0.5 *Enter King Leir, Skalliger, Perillus, and Nobles*] Lee: *Es treten auf der König Leir, Perillus, Skalliger, und Gefolge* Fischer.

    1. SP LEIR] Steevens+.

    1. Thus to] In accordance with.

        obsequies] funeral rites.

        perform'd] are performed; the omission of "are" was not unusual (Abbott, p. 290).

    2. too late] recently.

    3-4. heavenly joys . . . cherubins] (These terms are anachronistic since the play's setting is pre-Christian).

    4. cherubins] an early plural form of cherubim.

    6. princely] royal.

    10. wanting] lacking.

    13. Left] Are left (Abbott, p. 290).

        ship . . . stern] proverbial (Tilley S347 and W478).

    14. sheep . . . care] proverbial (Tilley S309 and S312).

    15. tender] cherish.

    20. And] But.

    25. earthly] earthy Hazlitt; *irdschen* Fischer.

    25. fain] willingly.

    31. bare] bore.

        quondam] former.

33. censure] judge.

35. jointer] jointure, marriage settlement.

39. unpartial] impartial.

   censure] judgment.

40. for me] "as far as regards me" (Nares, p. 324).

41. SP NOBLEMAN] this edition; *Nobles* Steevens, Lee; *Noble* Hazlitt, Fischer, Bullough.

42. indubitate] undoubted.

43. set] past tense of "sat" in sixteenth and seventeenth century English.

44. loose . . . life] release your life from its imprisoning body.

51. Albion] Britain.

54. sort] agree.

57. motion] propose.

60. allows] approves.

62. partial fancy] particular liking.

   hears] listens to.

74. Lest . . . swell] proverbial (Tilley S929).

76. sudden] unpremeditated.

81. vantage] opportunity, chance; literally, at the moment.

88. policy] strategy.

89. Brittany] a variant form of Britain. The playwright used two forms, Brittayne and Brittany, depending on whether he needed three syllables or two syllables to complete a line.

90. SD *für sich*] Fischer.

90. bewray] disclose.

   secrecy] secret.

91. *Alle ab bis auf Perillus*] Fischer.

202

91. Thus . . . beguile] proverbial (Tilley D179).

[Scene ii]

    0.1 Scene ii] MSR; Scene II, *A room in King Leir's palace* Lee; *Zweite Szene, Leirs Schloss* Fischer.

    2. peat] usually a term of endearment for a girl or woman, but here used ironically in the sense of "spoiled brat."

    5. quaint] clever, ingenious.

       soon] quickly.

    6. invention] devising.

    9. nice] refined.

    10. precise] scrupulous.

    15. desperate medicine] extreme remedy.

    17. prick] the highest position.

    18. And we . . . working days] And we will be treated as though we are ordinary and trivial.

    22. whenas] when.

    24. disgrace] lit., being out of favor; but what Ragan refers to here is that if Cordella marries before they do, she will have precedence over them even though they are older.

    25-6. prose Q+

       verse, lines end:

          she / me This edition.

    27. shirt] in undress, in a hurry, without formality or preparation.

    30-2. prose Q+

       verse, lines end:

          sister / Skalliger / import This edition.

    32.1 In line 32 Q.

    37. I am with child] I am very impatient; as a pregnant woman is impatient for the birth of her child. A common saying (Tilley C317).

45. doubts] fears.

50. so] if.

57. presently] immediately.

59. look whose] whatever person's (see Mark Eccles, "Shakespeare's Use of *Look How* and Similar Idioms," *JEGP*, 42 [1943], 386-400).

61. pleasing . . . voice] mermaids were often identified with the sirens of classical mythology, enchantresses whose sweet songs lured sailors to disaster.

66. enjoin] to bind by an oath.

69. Which] The which.

70. but] but that.

73.1 In line 73 Q

78. flatter with] flatter.

82. For why] Because.

88. will] it will.

97. grant to] grant.

98. Which] Which denial.

aggravate] intensify.

[Scene iii]

0.1 Scene iii] MSR; *Scene III, Presence chamber in King Leir's palace* Lee; *Dritte Szene, Leirs Schloss*.

8. dear regard] great importance.

12. toys] amusements.

13. annoys] annoyances.

17. affords] yields.

conformable] compliant.

18. presageth] forebodes.

30. assizes] a term associated with courts of law; here it refers specifically to judgment.

31. tender] cherish.

36. hest] behest.

40. rehears'd] uttered.

50. meanest] lowest.

55. SD *für sich*] Fischer.

61. forwardness] zealousness.

70. haply] perchance; may be a pun on happily too.

72. fancy] individual liking.

74. Philomel] nightingale.

75. SD *für sich*] Fischer.

78. paint] color.

80. look what] whatever.

83. brook] tolerate.

85. slight] weak.

86. minion] one specially favored or beloved.

89. As that] That.

92. short] shorten.

98. to this] to this point.

107-8. The praise . . . far off] A saying that is not traceable in any encyclopedia of proverbs; it probably means that since Gonorill lacks friends, she has to speak her own praises.

113. imp] child; used here as child of the devil, a demon.

114. tittle] tiniest bit; literally, a small stroke in handwriting.

117. nor] or Steevens.

120. to] for.

122. This done, because] When I have done this, so that.

125. presently] immediately.

126. pride . . . fall] proverbial (Tilley P581).

127. plain dealing] putting it plainly.

    sheen] resplendent.

128. You] Youd Fischer.

134. SD This edition.

135. lord thus fond] lord so foolish as.

[Scene iv]

    0.1 Scene iv] MSR; *Act II, Scene I The palace of the Gallian king* Lee; *Vierte Szene, Am Hof zu Frankreich* Fischer.

    2. flying fame] rumor.

    7. allow of] validate.

    10. seiz'd of] in legal possession of.

    11. Jason . . . fleece] Leader of the Argonauts, who, with the help of Medea, attained the golden fleece (See Ovid, *Metamorphoses*, VII).

    25. for] from.

    29. congees] salutations.

    42. palmer] pilgrim; properly, one from the Holy Land who bears a palm leaf as a symbol of his journey.

    weeds] garments.

    43. mistrust] be suspicious of.

    44. fit your turn] meet your requirements.

    45. Blunts] The name Mumford is a variant of the more familiar form Mountfort or Mountford. "The great Elizabethan family of the Blounts enjoyed the baronial title of Mountjoy to which a mysterious allusion is possibly made here" (Sidney Lee, ed., *The Chronicle History of King Leir: The Original of Shakespeare's 'King Lear'* [New York: Duffield and Company, 1909], pp. xxxiv-xxxv).

[Scene v]

    0.1 Scene v] MSR; *Scene II, On the road to King Leir's palace at Troynovant* Lee; *Fünfte Szenne, Auf der Kreusung zweier Landstrassen* Fischer.

5, 9, 13. SD's in margin Q.

14. at's] at his.

15. Daedalus' . . . wings] In Greek mythology Daedalus and his son Icarus fashioned wings of feathers and wax to escape the Labyrinth of Minos. They escaped successfully, but Icarus flew to near the sun causing the wax to melt. His wings fell from his shoulders, and he plunged into the sea (see Ovid, *Metamorphoses*, VIII).

17. Troynovant] New Troy, London.

25. slenderly accompanied] meagerly attended; Cornwall has only one servingman with him.

29. circumstances] detailed narrations.

35. letters] (plural but with a singular meaning).

38. of] Q, Hazlitt, Nichols, Fischer, Bullough; or MSR, Lee.

38. moiety] portion, share.

regiment] kingdom.

42. we . . . call] we must call each other brothers-in-law.

45. Ragan will] Ragan [he] will.

46. seigniories] revenues.

47-8. Whom . . . part] I would gladly have accepted Ragan even if only a third of the land was offered.

48. complements] qualities.

50. 'Zlood] 'sblood Lee.

50. 'Zlood] contraction of "God's blood."

62. For . . . intent] for fear that our delay may alter his intended purpose to divide the kingdom.

[Scene vi]

0.1 Scene vi] MSR; Scene III, *A room in King Leir's palace* Lee; *Sechste Szene, Leirs Schloss* Fischer.

3. sir-reverence] a corruption of "save your reverence," a mock apologetic phrase introducing a remark that might offend the hearer.

5. Since time] From the time.
warn'd] ordered.

207

10. reclaim'd again] reversed in his decision.

15. Beshrew] an imprecatory expression meaning "Evil befall" or "Devil take."

18. And clip . . . too high] proverbial (Tilley W498).

22. with nothing] without a penis.

27. benefice] a church living, often very modest.

27-8. She'll . . . gown] a contemptuous implication that Cordella is extravagant.

31. I think long] I am impatient.

43. kind] loving.

pelican] an emblem of self-sacrifice and parental devotion. The pelican, according to folklore, feeds her young with her own blood (P. Ansell Robin, *Animal Lore in English Literature* [London: Macmillan, 1932], p. 65.

45. jealous] watchful.

46. dazzle] "to lose distinctness of vision, especially from gazing at too bright light" (Onions).

45-7. And . . . sun] according to folklore, the eagle tests its young by forcing them to look steadily at the sun and kills one that cannot do so without watering eyes (Robin, p. 162).

48.1 In margin Q.

53. Priam] the last king of Troy.

55. for that] because.

56. was] were Lee.

65. Leander . . . Hero] A famous pair of tragic lovers of classical lore.

66. Aeneas . . . Carthage queen] Aeneas was a Trojan warrior who helped found Rome. Dido, the queen of Carthage, fell in love with him and committed suicide when he deserted her (see Ovid, *Metamorphoses*, XIV).

70. if welcome] if I am welcome.

78. resteth] remains.

81. SD *Zu den beiden Fürsten*] Fischer.

87. beads] devotions; literally, prayer beads.

97. doom] judgment.

99. and if] if.

105. lovely] loving.

110. strain forth] squeeze out; shed.

[Scene vii]

    0.1 Scene vii] MSR; *Scene IV, The open country in Britain* Lee; *Siebente Szene, Auf einer Landstrasse* Fischer.

    1. brook] like.

    2. told you of] warned against.

    humor] habit.

    7. 'Swounds] "By God's wounds."

    9. Trosillus] Tresillus Steevens+.

    9. Trosillus . . . Denapoll] These names appear to be the playwright's little pastoral jokes, since they have no significance otherwise.

    13. Jack] lit., a low-bred or ill-mannered fellow; Mumford is referring specifically to his blunders in addressing the king as a person of nobility.

    15. close] concealed.

    15.1 In margin Q; *Sie treten seitwarts* Fischer.

    17. SD *für sich*] Fischer.

    21. Queen of Chance] Goddess Fortune.

    21. pattern] example.

    22. imbecility] weakness.

28. embrace the rod] the rod as a symbol of authority and discipline is distinctly biblical in origin. Cf. "I will be his father, and he shall be my son; and if he sin, I will chasten him with the rod of men . . . " (II Samuel 7:14) and "Foolishness is bound in the heart of a child, but the rod of correction shall drive it away from him" (Proverbs 22:15).

    29-30. complain On] cry out against.

    30. unkindness] unnaturalness.

    33-5. *prose* this edition;

verse, lines end:
   hands / petticoat / together Q+.

35. shift . . . together] exchange; Mumford wants to undress with her.

38. Oh brave!] an interjection, meaning "Bravo!" "Excellent!"

   custom] business patronage or support.

39. St. Denis] the patron saint of France.

   sadly] solemnly.

39-40. I . . . wear] I agree to buy all my small clothes from her.

46. sempster] seamstress.

51.1 This edition.

60. silly] weak.

60-61. mouse . . . lion] from Aesop's fables. See also Tilley L315 and M1235.

64. hapless] unfortunate.

65. sometimes] formerly.

78. accept of] accept.

82. has any interest in my mind] has any claim on my judgment.

85. Except] Unless.

89. guise] manner

93. lusty] vigorous, but with added sense of handsome.

96. Hymen] the Greek and Roman god of marriage.

98. live] continue in life, as in the earlier phrase "Live the king" for "Long live the king."

102. Whilom whenas] Once when.

103. postulate] request.

105. light] fallen.

106. wise] wife Hazlitt.

106. surcease] stop.

107. whereas] where.

123. lovely] loving.

124. content] contentment.

126. Cordella, cordial . . . heart] The king puns on Cordella's name; a cordial is anything that invigorates and warms the heart.

129. unknown] strange.

140. sparks] indications. According to Elizabethan psychology, spark--the animating principle in man--is that trace of a quality in a person which cannot be disguised; in this case, it is the king's nobility.

141. weeds] garments.

145. wench] young woman.

146. exceptions] reservations in the oath.

147. foppets] foolish women.

150. resteth] remains.

152. because] so that.

158-60. *prose* this edition;

> *verse, lines end*:
>
>> live / ladies / France Q+.

158. except] unless.

159. humour] disposition.

[Scene viii]

0.1 Scene viii] MSR; *Act II, Scene I, A Road leading to Cornwall* Lee; *II.Act, Erste Szene, Gonorills Schloss* Fischer.

14. opprobrious sort] abusive way.

15. dotard] imbecile; but specifically from senility.

16. of] on.

18. iron age] the present age; a time of pain, sickness and oppression (Ovid, *Metamorphoses*, I).

19. contemned of] held in contempt by.

20. restrain'd] withheld.

24. alliance] kindred.

29. latest] last.

[Scene ix]

0.1 Scene ix] MSR; *Scene II, A room in the royal palace of Cornwall* Lee; *Zweite Szene, Gonorills Schloss* Fischer.

2. dignity] high rank.

3. peremptory] imperious.

4. doting] foolish.

5. of alms] by charity.

8. check] reprimand.

snap . . . up] make cutting remarks.

23. still] continually.

30. For why] Because.

30-31. For . . . spring] proverbial (Tilley A12 and W924).

[Scene x]

0.1 Scene x] MSR; *Scene III, A hall in the royal palace of Cornwall* Lee; *Dritte Szene, Gonorills Schloss* Fischer.

2. were wont] used to.

10.1 In lines 10-11 Q.

13. dumps] low spirits.

17. bread and cheese] figuratively, plain fare necessary to sustaining life; hard rations as punishment.

22. take an order] take steps; make arrangements.

24. partial] unduly favored.

28. touchy] irritable.

30. honest] chaste.

belike] in all likelihood.

34. For] To search out.

43. overlive myself] live past my time.

44. course . . . revers'd] unnaturalness; refers specifically to Gonorill's "unnatural" behavior towards her father.

in me] in my case.

45. wight] creature.

48.1 In line 48 Q.

49. SD This edition.

50. wasting] lavish.

65. Which] Who.

72. due revenues] income.

81. nature's . . . law] the law implanted by nature in the mind, a law capable of being demonstrated by human reason; specifically, the respect and honor his daughters owe him by virtue of his having given them life.

87. contemn] scorn.

103. entreat] treat.

[Scene xi]

0.1 Scene xi] MSR; *Scene IV, A room in the royal palace of Cambria* Lee; *Vierte Szene, Ragans Schloss* Fischer.

0.2 *solus*] *alone*; *sola* refers to females, whereas *solus* refers to males. The agreement of sex was not kept in stage directions either because of conventional phrasing or because boy actors made *sola* nonsense.

2. bodeth] decreed.

happy stars] the happy condition brought about by fortune.

4. event] outcome.

6. states] the classes of persons regarded as part of the body politic and as participating in the government--the nobles, clergy, and commonalty.

7. look whate'er] whatever. See note 59, scene ii, p. 101.

11. cooling card] a term of some unknown card game applied figuratively or punningly to anything that "cools" passions or enthusiasm.

13. quartermaster] literally, one who militarily exercises control over all matters related to the quartering, encamping, marching, and equipping of soldiers.

[Scene xii]

0.1 Scene xii] MSR; *Scene V, A Room in the royal palace of Cornwall* Lee; *Fünfte Szene, Gonorills Schloss* Fischer.

10. longest home] the grave.

18. frolic] merry.

22. SD *ab mit Gefolge*] Fischer

24. temper] to work upon; mould.

30. haply] perchance.

46. letters (See note 35, scene v,).

49.1 In line 49Q.

50-2. *prose* this edition;

    verse, lines end:
        Stand / be / letters Q+.

51. neck-verse] A Latin verse (usually the beginning of psalm 51) which was set before a criminal claiming benefit of clergy. If he could read it, he could save himself from trial in a secular court and could be tried in an ecclesiatical court which traditionally was more lenient than the secular court.

54-6. *prose* this edition;

    verse, lines end:
        I / up / him Q+.

57-8. He . . . degree] He that hangs thee or that but hurts thee in the least degree would fare better if he hanged his own father.

59. make . . . thee] have a high regard for you.

60. of] with.

76. set on it] determined.

77. Billinsgate] Billingsgate; one of the gates of the city of London and the fish market near it, the market noted for vituperative language. Foul language is itself called "billingsgate."

80. good cheap] bargains.

81. choler] anger.

82. razor ... Palermo] razor of the best quality.

89. other] i.e., letter.

91. detracted] disparaged.

94. commons] common people.

103-6. *prose* this edition;

>*verse, lines end*:
>done / will / poulter / skin Q+.

103. conceit] imagine; in other words, "consider it done."

105. poulter] one whose business is the sale of poultry and usually rabbits, as well as other small game.

cony] rabbit.

110. make ... away] put to death.

113.1 *Kiss*] *Kisses* Steevens.

113.1 *Kiss ... paper*] *Kissing the book was an act of oath-taking in a law court.*

[Scene xiii]

0.1 Scene xiii] MSR; *Act IV Scene I, Outside a church in Gallia* Lee; *Sechste Szene, Cordella Schloss* Fischer.

9. mirror ... time] model of excellence.

13. wish the thing] wish for anything.

want] lack.

18. pine] torment.

23. once] one day.

30. charity] love.

[Scene xiv]

0.2 *faintly*] *feebly*.

9. uncouth] unfamiliar.

12. guerdon] reward.

15. want] lack.

21. Whereas] Where.

23. gratify] to welcome.

31. SD *für sich*] Fischer.

31. of force] of necessity.

35. indurable] unendurable.

36. disaster] disastrous.

43.1 In margin Q.

44. finger in the eye] derisively used for "to weep". Cf. Tilley, F229.

53. upon a spleen] on a sudden impulse; but in particular, a splenetic one.

55. made on] fussed over.

[Scene xv]

0.1 Scene xv] MSR; *Scene III, Outside the royal palace of Cambria* Lee; III. *Akt, Erste Szene, Vor Ragans Schloss* Fischer.

4.1 In line 4 Q.

7. *Zu Ragan*] Fischer.

14. *für sich*] Fischer.

16. See] Steevens+; She Q.

17. dumb show] in early dramas, a part of a play represented by action without speech. See Dieter Mehl, *The Elizabethan Dumb Show* (Cambridge, Mass.: Harvard University Press, 1966), pp. 3-26.

19. crowns] coins with the value of five shillings each.

23. give out] proclaim.

24. list] desire.

28. make ... head] have him beheaded.

34. fact] actions.

39. his grace] i.e., the Duke, her husband.

41. cavillations] charges.

45. SD *Zum Boten*] Fischer.

53. compact] closely packed.

    adamant] the name of an alleged rock which was extremely hard.

56. respect] take into account.

62.1 SD *Gibt ihm eine Borse*] Fischer.

69. SD This edition.

[Scene xvi]

24. unkindly] contrary to nature.

27. present] presently.

28. pack] depart.

29-31. Not ... Doth] "Not" in line 29 modifies "Doth" in line 31; the line is read: That I miss my country or my kin ... doth not any whit ....

30. ancient] former.

31. distemperate] disorder.

37. stay] feed.

38. element] sky.

42-3. blackamoor ... skin] proverbial (Tilley E186).

44. Which all] All [of] which.

217

46. Mirror] see note 9, scene xiii, p. 229.

55. suffice the turn] serve the purpose.

64.1 SD This edition.

[Scene xvii]

  0.1 Scene xvii] MSR; *Scene V, A room in the royal palace of Cambria* Lee; *Dritte Szene, Vor Ragans Schloss* Fischer.

  1. It . . . world] It is a marvel.

  flush] plentifully supplied (with money).

  4. kiss . . . hands] pay their respects.

  6.1 In line 6 Q.

  9. and it like] may it please.

  13. dispatch'd] completed.

  17. by this] by now.

  22. that] that which.

  31. each . . . one] for each hand there is one victim.

  32.1 *Give*] *Gives* Steevens, Hazlitt, Lee, Fischer.

  35. So] If.

  46. mistrust] suspect.

  51. faint] weaken.

  53-4. pipe . . . Mercury] the messenger of the gods who rescued Io from Argus, her watchman with a hundred eyes, by playing on his pipe of reeds and by singing and telling stories until all the eyes of Argus were asleep (Ovid, *Metamorphoses*, I).

  54.1 In line 55 Q.

  57. dispatch'd] promptly concluded [the murders].

[Scene xviii]

  0.1 Scene xviii] MSR; *Scene VI, A room in the royal palace of Cornwall* Lee; *Vierte Szene, Gonorills Schloss* Fischer.

1. stay] tarry.

9. therefor] for that [reason].

13. And't] If it.

15. SD *Zu Gonorill*] Fischer.

15. message] errand.

18. SD *Zum Diener*] Fischer.

36. SD *Zum Gesandten*] Fischer.

36. had in charge] was commanded.

49. On three lines in Q; they can be scanned as one line.

54. expiate] end.

56. exasperate] increase the fierceness of.

66. SD In margin Q.

[Scene xix]

0.1 Scene xix] MSR; *Scene VII, In the open country of Cambria* Lee; *Fünfte Szene, Wilder Wald* Fischer.

2. 'Tis news] It is a novelty.

rathe] early in the day.

3. heavy] sleepy.

6. use to do] are accustomed to.

8.1 *Pull . . . sit*] *Pulls . . . sits* Steevens, Lee.

10. "good fellows"] robbers.

12. in good case] in trouble.

13. stand . . . hands] to rely upon our hands for our defense.

16. Even] Just.

21-2. rob-thief] robber.

22. perforce] by force

24. graybeards] contemptuous reference to old men.

29. provided] equipped.

30. bravely] valiantly.

34. But that] Except.

36. Mass] an abbreviation of "By the Mass," used as an oath.

38. marvel] wonder.

40. miscarry] come to harm.

43. dreams] Many Elizabethans believed that dreams were often omens of some calamity for the dreamer or those near him (see Tilley D587).

45. SD *seitwärts*] Fischer.

47. effect] outcome.

48. pretends] signifies.

49. SD *seitwärts*] Fischer.

51. aspects] looks.

52. hand] hands Lee.

52. falchion] a short, slightly curved sword.

54. poniard] dagger.

58. balsam] an aromatic medicine for healing wounds.

63. yet] still.

64. SD This edition.

64. presently] immediately.

65. SD This edition.

65. Stand] Stop.

65.1 In line 65 Q.

66. *reel*] whirl around.

much ado] great difficulty.

67. Deliver] Surrender.

68. Deliver . . . Lord] echo of the litany service, *The First and Second Prayer Books of King Edward VI* (New York: Dutton, 1964), pp. 231-2, 361-2.

71. faithful watchmen] a mocking reference to Leir and Perillus who, like Jesus' disciples, could not stay awake and watch. This reference is echoed again in line 76 below, "watch and pray."

72. halberds] a military weapon; a combination of spear and battleax. But here the messenger mocks Leir and Perillus by referring to their useless books as halberds.

73. want] lack.

73.1 *Show*] *Shows* Steevens, Lee.

75. stay] staying power.

76. watch and pray] Cf. "Take heed; watch and pray, for ye know not when the time is" (Mark 13:33). See also Matthew 26:41 and Mark 14:38.

77. proper] respectable.

81. That . . . false] That that is false.

82. that] what.

83.1 In line 83 Q.

   Take it] *Takes it* Steevens; *The messenger takes it* Lee.

85.1 *Take . . . hands*] *The messenger takes his, and weighs them both in his hands* Lee.

88. use me] employ me or my name to your advantage.

89. pleasure thee] do you a favor.

94.1 *Proffer*] *Proffers* Lee.

   In line 94 Q.

97. vantage] position of strength.

98. try this gear] test all this talk.

104. SP AMBO] Both.

104.1 In line 104 Q.

107. dispatch'd] killed.

119. Damon] In Roman mythology, Damon and Pythias were two friends so devoted to each other that Damon pledged his life as a hostage for the condemned Pythias.

124, 128. of purpose] on purpose (see Abbott, p. 115).

127. short] shorten; the use of short as a verb was common.

129. 'Zoons] By God's wounds.

133. SD *auf sein Gesicht deutend*] Fischer.

134. fashion] shape.

147. Whether] Whither.

156. except] excepted.

158. heaven's bright eye] the sun.

160. sure] assuredly.

thou . . . mark] you are mistaken; literally, mark is the object aimed at in throwing or shooting.

168. In . . . world] In Christian love with your fellowman.

But now] Only this moment.

191. and if] if.

192. SD This edition.

195.1 This edition.

198. prosecute] continue.

201. pass'd] pledged.

203.1 *bless themselves*] *make the sign of the cross.*

208. viperous generation] Cf. "Oh generation of vipers, how can you speak good things when ye are evil?" (Matthew 12:30).

212. SD *Zum Boten*] Fischer.

216. SD *für sich*] Fischer.

217. SD *zu Perillus.*

220, 222. latest] last.

223. Withal] With this.

desire] ask.

226. *Zum Boten*] Fischer.

235. presently] immediately.

237. ride post] ride as a courier.

237.1 *Show*] *Shows* Steevens, Lee.

244. skilleth not] matters not.

250. high anointed of the Lord] a king by divine right; Perillus is appealing to the murderer to beware laying hands upon the king who has been anointed as God's deputy on earth. He is refering to the tradition, stemming from the Old Testament, that to do violence upon the person of the king is a grievous crime against God as well as man, and one which will not go unpunished. Cf. "And David said to Abishai, Destroy him [Saul] not; for who can lay his hand on the Lord's anointed and be guiltless?" (I Samuel 26:9); see also II Samuel 1:14 -16, I Chronicles 16:22; and Psalms 105:15. This tradition of the consecrated king was very much alive in the 1590's, e.g., in Shakespeare, *Richard II* (III.ii.54-7).

260-1. I . . . company] I brought him here where he would not have been now, if he had not chosen out of his good will to keep me company.

272.1 In line 272 Q.

275. SD This edition.

281. have . . . presently] have not [gold] presently.

283. still] always.

298. The King . . . mind] "May the King . . . "

299. stay'st] hesitate.

301. I . . . me] I will not do it though now you do entreat me to do so.

303. Beshrew] "Evil befall you" or "Devil take you."

304. parlousest] most cunning or dangerous; the superlative of "parlous" which is a contraction of "perilous."

305. flat] plain.

308.1 In margin Q.

310. It shall . . . thee re-greet] i.e., It shall prove to your disadvantage when we meet again.

311. overpast] past.

312. hie] hasten.

326. charity] Christian love.

328. What time] At the time when.

335. tried] tested.

341. kinder] more loving.

[Scene xx]

    0.1 Scene xx] MSR; *Scene VIII. Outside the royal palace of Cornwall* Lee; *IV. Akt, Erste Szene, Gonorills Schloss* Fischer.

    6. hither] i.e., Gonorill's castle.

    11-14. *prose* this edition;

        verse, lines end:

            again / wench / forsworn / live Q+.

    11. fain] gladly.

    12. import] mean.

[Scene xxi]

    0.1 Scene xxi] MSR; *Act V, Scene I. A room in the royal palace of Gallia* Lee; *Zweite Szene, Cordellas Schloss* Fischer.

    1. By this] By now.

    3. presageth] foretells.

    13. forsworn] falsely sworn.

    16-8. *prose* this edition;

        verse, lines end:
            one / her Q+.

    17. at all adventures] at any risk.

    20-2. *prose* this edition;

> *verse, lines end*:
> it / days / France Q+.

23-7. *prose* this edition;

> *verse, lines end*:
> you / she / you / man / do Q+.

28-9. *prose* this edition;

> *verse, lines end*:
> nonce / mocks Q+.

28. slops] baggy hose.

29. mocks] taunts.

32. bobs] taunts.

33. bombast] cotton wool used specifically for padding hose or slops.

35. outface] out do.

36. my mistress' quarrel] my claim to my mistress.

39-40. cart . . . wench] prostitutions were chastised publicly by being carted through the streets.

41. give . . . over] give up on you; lit., yield.

51. very now] at this moment.

51-2. go in progress] travel.

54. motion] proposal.

55.1 This edition.

56. match . . . forward] decision (to go to the seashore) be carried out.

58. needs not] is not necessary.

59. So] If.

63. make one] disguise.

71. You . . . first] You shall be our master.

72. 'Twere more than time] It's about time!

[Scene xxii]

0.1 Scene xxii] MSR; *Scene II, A room in the royal palace of Cambria* Lee; *Dritte Szene, Ragans Schloss* Fischer.

5. light-horse] light-armed cavalry.

6. regiment] kingdom.

14. SD *auf das Gefolge weisend*] Fischer.

15. loss] Lee, Bullough; less Q, Steevens, Hazlitt, Fischer; a misprint in the quarto which the other editors mistakenly followed.

17. sense] reason.

18. in . . . enter] can even engage in the consideration of the cause.

22. innovation] alteration (for the worse).

23. timeless] prematurely.

35. patience] endurance.

52. packing] underhanded plotting.

57. color] disguise.

66. law of arms] literally, the recognized custom of professional soldiers; but in this line, the term is used in the sense of diplomatic immunity afforded the representative of another government, forbidding any mistreatment of that person.

75. ill-beseeming] ill-befitting.

76. mere] entire.

   tender] owe.

77. respected] valued.

81. enforce] emphasize.

82. doubtful] apprehensive.

83. And that] (This phrase is used to introduce a clause which amplifies the previous clause.)

86. mate] fellow.

86.1 In margin Q.

90.1 In line 90 Q.

94.1 In line 94 Q.

95-6. Infringe . . . obloquy] To break the law of arms would be to my everlasting disgrace.

99. put up] allow.

100. is made away] has been killed.

106. after-ages] posterity.

    admire] marvel at.

110. best occasion] best [as] occasion.

[Scene xxiii]

    0.1 Scene xxiii] MSR; *Scene III, A port on the coast of Cambria* Lee; *Vierte Szene, Am Meerestramd Frankreichs* Fischer.

    0.2 SD *sea-gowns and sea-caps*] Seamen of the time wore very full baggy breeches gathered in below the knee, loose waist length coats with slits and lace holes in front at the neck. They also wore shaggy, brimless hats which were flat and round (Phillis Cunnington and Catherine Lucas, *Occupational Costume in England* [London: A. and C. Black Co., 1967], pp. 55-6).

5. good fellows] (See note 10, scene xix).

9. mean] meantime.

11. *Look*] *Looks* Steevens, Lee.

    SD in line 10 Q.

13. *Look*] *Looks* Steevens, Lee.

    SD in line 12 Q.

13. marvel] wonder.

14. room] place.

15. mean] inferior.

17. stand to do] resist doing.

20-1. forgive . . . passage] remit the cost of your passage.

22.1 In line 22 Q.

    changeth] *change* Lee.

23. SD this edition.

25. sheep's russet] wool.

    bide . . . stress] withstand . . . strain.

26. Yet] Lee, Bullough; Yes Steevens, Hazlitt; *Ja* Fischer.

27.1 *Pull*] *Pulls* Steevens, Lee

30. but would] If only.

31. SD *Zum ersten Matrosen*] Fischer.

31. doublet] a close fitting upper body garment.

33. powder'd beef] beef preserved by salting or pickling.

38. *Leir to Perillus* in line 38 Q.

    SD *Zum ersten Matrosen*] Fischer.

39. SD *zu Leir*] Fischer.

41-3. *prose* this edition;

    verse, lines end:
        together / anon / well Q+.

45. I'll . . . another] I'll cheat you as I would another person.

46-7. *prose* this edition;

    verse, lines end:
        money / again Q+.

56. or ever] before.

59. henbane] common name of the plant *Hyoscyamus niger*, having an unpleasant smell, and narcotic as well as poisonous properties.

    mithridate] a composition of many ingredients in the form of a pleasant tasting substance, regarded as a universal antidote or preservative against poison and infectious disease. Named for Mithridates, king of Pontus, who successfully avoided every attempt to poison him by prudent anticipation.

60. wormwood] the plant *Artemisia absinthium*, proverbial for its bitter taste.

63. sugar'd] precious.

66. envious] malicious.

prick'd . . . heart] an allusion to the nightingale that, according to tradition, sings while holding a thorn to its breast (Tilley N183).

68. respectless] reckless.

73. go . . . aslope] slip away.

84. crosses] misfortunes.

86-9. The worst . . . thousand deaths] The worst that can happen is death, yet death is better than despair. Risk death; by doing so you may attain new life, for death may not come at all. But banish despair, since it brings nothing except all the fears attendant on death (see Tilley, C774). Cf. Shakespeare, *Julius Caesar*: "Cowards die many times before their death; / The valiant never taste of death but once" (II.ii.32).

94. apaid] requited.

[Scene xxiv]

0.1 Scene xxiv] MSR; *Scene IV, The open country near the coast of Gallia* Lee; *Fünfte Szene, Freundlicher Wald mit Lichtun* Fischer.

11. quirks] peculiar behavior.

beyond the moon] to extravagant lengths.

12. take on them] pretend.

antic] bizarre.

16.1 In margin Q.

16.1 *faintly*] *feebly*.

18. o'ergone] overcome.

20. SD *König, Königin und Mumford treten seitlich* Fischer.

28. betide unto] befall.

33.1 In line 33 Q.

33.1 *He . . . arms*] *He pushes up his sleeves*.

35. virtue] a particular power inherent in physical things (in this case, blood) that strengthens, nourishes, and heals.

38. cann'ball] this edition; camball Q; Caniball Steevens, Hazlitt, Fischer, Bullough; cannibal Lee.

38. cann'ball] cannibal.

48. SD This edition.

64. occasion] reason.

65. of all] especially.

71. ground] basis.

73.1 This edition.

75. Or . . . or] Either . . . or.

76. SD *Er kommt nach vorne*] Fischer.

85. Vouchsafe] Graciously consent.

86. SD In margin Q.

89.1 In line 89 Q.

90. say grace] say a grace Steevens, Lee.

91. sauce . . . stomach] proverbial (Tilley S96).

94.1 In margin Q.

96. Aeson] the aged father of Jason, leader of the Argonauts. At Jason's request, Medea, his wife and a sorceress, restored Aeson to youthfulness by her charms (Ovid, *Metamorphoses*, VII).

99. Elias] Elijah, a Hebrew prophet. The incident referred to is in I Kings 19:8. "Then he [Elijah] arose, and did eat and drink, and walked in the strength of that meat forty days and forty nights unto Horeb the mount of God."

105. office] function.

109-10. Manna . . . Israelites] Cf. "And had rained down manna upon them for to eat, and had given them of the wheat of heaven" (Psalms 78:24); see also Exodus 16:15-35.

113. congratulate] gratefully acknowledge.

116. requital] recompense.

121. unaquainted] unfamiliar.

127, 128. owe] possess.

129. interest] claim.

134. him list] he chooses.

136. I . . . had] I have two more daughters than I wish I had.

148. sped] well endowed.

158. Might] Is able to; "might" is the past tense of "may," which in sixteenth and seventeenth century English could mean "having the ability or power."

166. entreated] treated.

175. fain] "glad under the circumstances" (Onions).

to repair] to go.

178. sore] harsh.

180. betime] early.

182. 'Pointing] Appointing.

183. shag-hair'd] (a costume and make-up direction in the text).

196. what] who.

204.1 In line 204 Q.

206.1 In line 206 Q.

208.1 In line 208 Q.

210. resign'd] given.

210.1 In line 210 Q.

211. the word beseems not me] It is not befitting for me (to pardon you).

221. world] the earth and all its inhabitants.

223. SP KING.] PER. Bullough; Bullough acknowledges his change in a footnote, but he gives no reason for it. The speech properly belongs to the king of France.

225.1 In line 225 Q.

226. respective] respectful.

228.1 In line 228 Q.

232-33. blessing . . . Judah] Cf. "And I will make of thee a great nation, and will bless thee, and make thy name great, and thou shalt be a blessing" (Genesis 12:2).

237.1 In line 237 Q.

248.1 In line 248 Q.

251. sect] a particular group of persons.

254.1 *Rise*] *Rises* Steevens, Lee.

　　　In line 254 Q.

255. SD *Er kniet nieder*] Fischer

255.1 In lines 255-6 Q.

259.1 In line 259 Q.

　　　Rise] *Rises* Steevens, Lee.

[Scene xxv]

　　　0.1 Scene xxv] MSR; *Scene V, Ragan's royal palace of Cambria* Lee; *V. Akt. Erste Szene. Ragans Schloss* Fischer.

　　　0.2 *sola*] (See note 0.2, scene xi).

　　　2. fact] action.

　　　7. Make . . . sure] kill.

　　　13. white liver'd] having, according to an old notion, a light colored liver, supposed to be due to a deficiency of bile, and hence of vigor, spirit, or courage.

　　　17. mere] pure.

　　　22. heartless] cowardly.

　　　23. pox] name for several different diseases characterized by "pocks" or eruptive pustules on the skin; but "pox" usually refers specifically to syphilis.

　　　29. make . . . shift] devise a stratagem.

　　　　　for one] "to save my life" (Onions).

　　　30. repines] complains.

[Scene xxvi]

　　　0.1 Scene xxvi] MSR; *Scene VI, A Port of Gallia* Lee; *Zweite Am Meeresufer Frankreichs* Fischer.

11. wight] man.

12. meanest] of the lowest rank.

13. second] support.

15. next . . . ourself] second only to me.

16. not doubting of] with no feeling of uncertainty.

17. wonted] usual.

19. magnamity] lofty courage.

22. SD *Auf Cordella zeigend*] Fischer.

22. sweet saint] St. Denis, patron saint of France.

29. Genovestan Gauls] Gauls from Genoa, Italy, hardly seems likely; the playwright probably meant Cenouenses Galli. "Warner in his *Albion's England* Bk. III. ch. xvi., in describing the exploits in France of Bren or Brennus, a successor of Lear on the British throne, mentioned that Bren's allies in Gual were 'the Cenouesean Gawles.' Doubtless the old dramatist there found the word, which his printer reproduced as Genouestan . . . . . Orleans, the city of mid France, seems to have been originally called Cenabum or Genabum, and its inhabitants Cenabenses or Genabenses" (Lee, *King Leir*, p. 117).

30. Redshanks] a puzzling reference since Redshanks is "a designation commonly applied by Elizabethan writers only to Irish Celts or Gaelic Scots, from their habit of going bare-legged" (Lee, *King Leir*, p. 117). Mumford, however, gives his own reason in line 31 for calling his men Redshanks.

32. right] proper.

35. shot] a soldier armed with a firearm.

36. halberds] a soldier armed with a halberd which is a combination of spear and battle-ax.

bills] halberds.

[Scene xxvii]

0.1 Scene xxvii] MSR; *Scene VII, The ramparts of a town in Britain (Dover)* Lee; *Dritte Szene, An der brittischen Kuste* Fischer.

SD *Vorne links ein Hugel mit einer Signalkanone. Rechts im Hintergrund ein Teil vom Stadtwall mit einem Ausfalltor* Fischer.

1. *Bild. Aug dem Hügel erscheint im Hauptmann der Stadtwache mit zwei Wächtern* Fischer.

5. fire] light.

7. SD *Hinter dem Hauptmann herredend*] Fischer.

8. SD *Zum andern Wächter*] Fischer.

12. goodman] host (of an inn).

14-5. then so] let it be so.

17. excuse] malapropism for "accuse."

20. by craft] deceitfully (by a cunning use of language).

28. as much to say] as much as to say Lee.

28. conster] construe.

[Scene xxviii]

0.1 Scene xxviii] MSR; *Scene VIII, Before the walls of a town in Britain (Dover)* Lee; *2. Bild, Es ziehn aus von der rechten Seite her der König von Gallian und Mumford an der Spitze des Heers im schweigendem Zug* Fischer.

0.2 *still*] muffled drumbeat.

1. ensigns] banners.

5. mistrustful] suspicious.

9. pretend] portend.

[Scene xxix]

0.1 Scene xxix] MSR; *Scene IX, An open place in a town of Britain* Lee; *3. Bild, Im Hintergrund Wässenlarm des Überfalls. Aus dem aufgeriffenen Stadttor Stürzen zwei Haupleute der Stadtwache hervor. Hinter ihnen im Torweg eine wildbewegte Gruppe halbnachter Männer und Frauen. Zwei Hauptleute--ohne Wams, das Schwert in der Hand--rennen nach dem Hugel mit der Alarmkanone* Fischer.

0.2 SD *Alarum*] Peal of a warning bell.

14.1 In line 14 Q.

17.1 In line 17 Q.

(Er zieht vom Leder, um sie niederzustechen.) Es stürmt Mumford heran mit blossem Schwert. Die Hauptleute rennen davon Fischer.

18.1 In line 18 Q.

20. lack] want.

21. meanspace] meantime.

22. tall] valiant.

25. choler] anger.

27. and] if.

27.1 Scene xxx MSR; *Scene X, An open place in a town of Britain* Lee; *4. Bild. Kampfgetöse im Innern der Stadt. Aus dem Tor drängen sich Fluchtende, eiliche halbnacht. Hinter ihnen Mumford, der sie Versprengt. Dahn Ruhe. Zuletzt kommen aus dem Tor in langem Zuge der König von Gallien, Leir, Mumford, Cordella mit einer Schaar von Kriegern--inmitten die Ratshern der Stadt, gefesselt* Fischer.

27.1 *excursions*] running about.

30. revoke . . . from] renounce your allegiance to.

33. in justice of] in conformity to the moral rights of.

35. So] Provided that.

36. perforce] of necessity.

44. Which] i.e., people of the country.

45. their] i.e., of Cambria, Cornwall, Ragan, and Gonorill.

47. apace] quickly.

50. adventured . . . blood] risked your life.

51. Without . . . good] To do me so much good without my deserving it.

56. wont] accustomed.

61. foil] defeat.

64. amplify] increase the importance (of the coming battle).

65.1 In line 65 Q.

66. adverse drum] the drums of the opposing army.

67. St. Denis and St. George] patron saints of France and England respectively.

67.1 *Es kommen an der Spitze ihres Heeres Cornwall, Cambrien, Gonorill, und Ragan--von aussen link*] Fischer.

76. fell] savage.

84. Except] Unless.

84-5. Except . . . lands] Unless . . . you run to the sea perceiving you're lost on the land.

86. ferret] hunt and drive out.

87. crake] boast; also, croak.

90. color's sake] for a pretext.

91. set a gloss] give a fair appearance.

97. stark naught] utterly evil.

98. Anon] Straightway.

105.1 In line 105 Q.

110. of] Steevens+; or Q.

116. mean] intend.

119. betimes] at an early hour.

121. latter day] end of the world.

131. brawling] quarreling.

131.1 Scene xxxi] MSR; *Scene XI, A Battlefield outside the walls of a town of Britain* Lee; *5. Bild. Schlactlarm. Ein Teil des Gesechts zieht sich dann über die Buhne hin. Man sieht, wie Cambrien von Mumford verfolgt wird. Die Buhne wirde wieder leer. Nun kommt Cornwall allein und erschopft* Fischer.

136. *Uber die Buhne ziehen Fluchtende. Als letzter Cambrien* Fischer.

138.1 In line 138 Q.

140. give . . . due] treat you with justice.

144. set . . . heart] graft them onto [someone] with a better heart.

144.1 Scene xxxii] MSR; *Scene XII, The same* Lee; *6. Bild. Neuerlicher Schlachtgetümmel zieht über die Bühne. Dann von ferne und immer häher Victoriarufen. Englich treten auf Leir, Perillus, der König von Gallien und krugerisches Gefolge* Fischer.

144.1 *sound victory*] *proclaiming by trumpet, or other instrument, triumph over the enemy.*

154. ventured] risked.

scathe] harm.

158. grutch] complain.

162. unkind] ungrateful.

171. laid on] assaulted.

175. SD *Er reicht Cordella und dem König die Hands* Fischer.

BIBLIOGRAPHY

A List of Works Consulted

Abbott, E. W. *A Shakespearian Grammar*. 3rd ed., 1870; rpt. New York: Dover Publications, Inc., 1966.

Alexander, Peter. *Shakespeare's Life and Art*. New York: New York University Press, 1967.

Arber, Edward, ed. *A Transcript of the Registers of the Company of Stationers of London:1554-1640*. 5 vols. London: (Privately Printed), 1875-77. New York: P. Smith, 1950.

Barton, Anne. "The King Disguised: Shakespeare's *Henry V* and the Comical History." *The Triple Bond*. Ed. Joseph G. Price. University Park, Penn.: Pennsylvania State University Press, 1941.

Bentley, Gerald Eades. *The Jacobean and Caroline Stage*. 6 vols. Oxford: The Clarendon Press, 1975.

Bowers, Fredson. "Bibliographical Evidence from the Printer's Measure." *Studies in Bibliography*, 2 (1949-50), 153-167.

-------. "Elizabethan Proofing," *J.Q. Adams Memorial Studies*. Ed. J. G. McManaway, E. Giles, and E. E. Willoughby. Washington: The Folger Library, 1948.

-------. *On Editing Shakespeare and the Elizabethan Dramatists*. Philadelphia: University of Pennsylvania Press, 1955.

-------. *Principles of Bibliographical Description*. New York: Russell and Russell, 1962.

-------. "Some Relations of Bibliography to Editorial Problems." *Studies in Bibliography*, 3 (1950), 37-62.

-------. *Textual Study and Literary Criticism*. Cambridge: Cambridge University Press, 1959.

Bradbrook, Muriel C. *Themes and Conventions of Elizabethan Tragedy*. Cambridge: Cambridge University Press, 1935.

Bullough, Geoffrey. *Narrative and Dramatic Sources of Shakespeare*. 7 vols. New York: Columbia University Press, 1973.

Bullough, Goeffrey. "*King Lear* and the Annesley Case." *Festschrift: Rudolf Stamm*. Berne, Switzerland, 1969. pp. 43-50.

Capell, Edward. *Mr. William Shakespeare His Comedies, Histories, and Tragedies*. 10 vols. London: Henry Hughes, 1767-68.

Chambers, E. K. *The Elizabethan Stage*. 4 vols. Oxford: The Clarendon Press, 1923.

The Chronicle History of King Leir: The Original of Shakespeare's 'King Lear.' Ed. Sidney Lee. The Shakespeare Library. New York: Duffield and Co., 1909.

Clemen, Wolfgang. *English Tragedy Before Shakespeare*. Trans. T.S. Dorsch. London: Methuen and Co., 1961.

Collier, J. Payne. *A Bibliographical and Critical Account of the Rarest Books in the English Language*. 4 vols. London: J. Murray, 1866.

-------. *A History of English Dramatic Poetry to the Time of Shakespeare*. 3 vols. London: J. Murray, 1831.

-------. *The Plays of Shakespeare*. London: Whittaker and Co., 1842-4.

Craig, Hardin. *The Complete Works of Shakespeare*. New York: Scott, Foresman and Co., 1951.

Cunningham, Peter. *Extracts from the Accounts of the Revels at Court, in the Reigns of Queen Elizabeth and James I, from the Original Office Books of the Masters and Yeomen*. London: Shakespeare Society Publication, 1842.

Cunnington, Phillis and Catherine Lucas. *Occupational Costume in England*. London: A. and C. Black Co., 1967.

A Dictionary of Printers and Booksellers in England, Scotland and Ireland and of Foreign Printers of English Books, 1557-1640. Ed. R.B. McKerrow, London: Clarendon Press, 1910.

Documents Relating to the Office of the Revels in the Time of Queen Elizabeth. Ed. Albert Feuillerat. Vanduz: Kraus, 1963.

Doran, Madeleine. "Elements in the Composition of *King Lear*." *Studies in Philology*, 30 (1933), 34-58.

-------. *Endeavors of Art*. Madison: University of Wisconsin Press, 1954.

Dyce, Alexander. *The Works of Shakespeare.* 8 vols. London: Chapman and Hall, 1864-7.

Eccles, Mark. "Shakespeare's Use of *Look How* and Similar Idioms." JEGP, 42 (1943), 386-400.

Elizabethan Dramatists other than Shakespeare. Ed. Ernest H. C. Oliphant. New York: Printice Hall, 1931.

The Elizabethan Underworld. Ed. A.V. Judges. London: Routledge and Kegan Paul, 1930.

The First and Second Prayer Books of King Edward VI. Intro. E.C.S. Gibson. New York: Dutton, 1964.

Fleay, Frederick G. *A Biographical Chronicle of the English Drama, 1559-1642.* 2 vols. London: Reeves and Turner, 1891.

-------. *A Chronicle History of the Life and Works of William Shakespeare, Player, Poet, and Play Maker.* London: J.C. Nimmo, 1886.

Furness, H.H. *A New Variorum Edition of the Works of Shakespeare: King Lear.* Philadelphia: J.P. Lippincott Co., 1908.

Gaskell, Philip. *A New Introduction to Bibliography.* Oxford: Clarendon Press, 1972.

The Geneva Bible: A Facsimile of the 1560 Edition. Intro. Lloyd E. Berry. Madison, Wisconsin: University of Wisconsin Press, 1969.

Greg, W.W. *A Bibliography of the English Printed Drama to the Restoration.* 4 vols. London: The Bibliographical Society, 1939-1959.

-------. "The Date of *King Lear* and Shakespeare's Use of Earlier Versions of the Story." *Library*, 20 (1940), 377-400.

-------. *Dramatic Documents from the Elizabethan Playhouses.* 2 vols. Oxford: Clarendon Press, 1931.

-------. *The Editorial Problem in Shakespeare.* Oxford: Clarendon Press, 1967.

-------. *A List of English Plays Written before 1643 and Printed before 1700.* London: The Bibliographical Society, 1900.

-------. *The Shakespeare First Folio.* Oxford: Clarendon Press, 1955.

-------. *Some Aspects and Problems of London Publishing Between 1550 and 1650*. Oxford: Clarendon Press, 1956.

Harbage, Alfred B. *Annals of Engligh Drama, 975-1700*. Rev. Samuel Schoenbaum. London: Methuen, 1964.

-------. *Shakespeare and the Rival Traditions*. New York: Macmillan, 1952.

Hazlitt, W. Carew. *The English Drama and Stage under the Tudor and Stuart Princes, 1543-1664: Illustrated by a Series of Documents, Treaties, and Poems*. London: The Roxburghe Library, 1869.

-------. *Handbook to the Popular, Poetical, and Dramatic Literature of Great Britian from the Invention of Printing to the Restoration*. London: J.R. Smith, 1867.

Henslowe, Phillip. *Henslowe's Diary*. Ed. R.A. Foakes and R.T. Rickert. Cambridge: Cambridge University Press, 1961.

-------. *Henslowe's Diary*. Ed. W.W. Greg. 2 vols. London: A.H. Bullen, 1904-8.

Hinman, Charlton. "Cast-Off Copy for the First Folio of Shakespeare." *Shakespeare Quarterly*, 6 (1955), 257-273.

------------------. "The Prentice Hand in the Tragedies of the Shakespeare First Folio: Compositor E." *Studies in Bibliography*, 9 (1957), 3-20.

-------. "The Principle Governing the use of Variant Spellings as Evidence of Alternate Setting by Two Compositors." *Library* 21 (1941), 78-94.

-------. *The Printing and Proof-Reading of the First Folio of Shakespeare*. 2 vols. Oxford: Clarendon Press, 1963.

The History of King Leir 1605. Ed. W.W. Greg. Malone Society Reprint. Oxford: Oxford University Press, 1907.

Holzknecht, Karl. *The Backgrounds of Shakespeare's Plays*. New York: American Book Company, 1950.

Hudson, Henry N. *The Works of Shakespeare*. 11 vols. Boston: J. Munroe and Co., 1851-7.

Jewkes, Wilfred T. *Act Division in Elizabethan and Jacobean Plays 1583-1616*. Hamden, Conn.: The Shoestring Press, 1958.

Knight, Charles. *Pictorial Edition of the Works of Shakespeare*. New York: P.F. Collier, 1838.

Law, R.A. "*King Leir* and *King Lear*: An examination of the Two Plays." *Studies in Honor of T.W. Baldwin*. Ed. Don C. Allen. Urbana: University of Illinois Press, 1958. pp. 112-124.

Lewis, C.S. *English Literature in the Sixteenth Century Excluding Drama*. Oxford: Clarendon Press, 1944.

McKenzie, D.F. "Printers of the Mind: Some Notes on Bibliographical Theories and Printing-House Practices." *Studies in Bibliography*, 22 (1969), 1-75.

McKerrow, R.B. "The Elizabethan Printer and Dramatic Manuscripts." *Library*, 12 (1931), 253-75.

-------. *An Introduction to Bibliography*. Oxford: Clarendon Press, 1957.

Mehl, Dieter. *The Elizabethan Dumb Show*. Cambridge, Mass.: Harvard University Press, 1966.

The Mirror for Magistrates. Ed. Lily B. Campbell. New York: Barnes and Noble, 1960.

Moxon, Joseph. *Mechanick Exercises*. Ed. H. Davis and H. Carter. London, 1962.

Muir, Kenneth. *Shakespeare's Sources*. London: Methuen and Co., 1957.

Murray, John T. *English Dramatic Companies 1558-1642*. 2 vols. Boston: Houghton Mifflin, 1910.

Nares, Robert. *A Glossary of Words, Phrases, Names and Allusions*. Ed. James O. Halliwell and Thomas Wright. 2 vols. London, 1867.

Oliphant, Ernest H.C. *Shakespeare and his Fellow Dramatists*. 2 vols. New York: Prentice Hall, 1921.

Onions, C.T. *A Shakespeare Glossary*. 2nd ed., 1911; rpt, Oxford: Clarendon Press, 1951.

Ovidius Naso, Publius. *Metamorphoses*. Trans. Rolfe Humphries. Bloomington, Indiana: Indiana University Press, 1958.

Oxford English Dictionary. Ed. James A.H. Murray, *et al*. 12 vols. Oxford: Oxford University Press, 1884-1928.

Parts Added to The Mirror for Magistrates. Ed. Lily B. Campbell. Cambridge: Cambridge University Press, 1946.

Perritt, W. *The Story of King Lear from Geoffrey of Monmouth to Shakespeare*. Berlin: Mayer and Muller, 1904.

The Plays of William Shakespeare. Second edition, rev. and augmented by Isaac Reed. London: C. Bathurst, 1778.

Plomer, Henry R. *A Dictionary of the Booksellers and Printers Who Were at Work in England, Scotland and Ireland from 1641-1667*. Oxford: Clarendon Press, 1968.

Pollard, A.W. *Shakespeare's Fight with the Pirates*. Cambridge: Cambridge University Press, 1915.

-------. and G.R. Redgrave, eds. *A Short-Title Catalogue of Books Printed in England, Scotland, and Ireland*. London: The Bibliographical Society, 1926.

Quellen zu König Lear. Ed. Rudolf Fischer. Shakespeares Quellen. Bonn: A. Marcus and E. Weber Verlag, 1914.

Ribner, Irving. *The English History Play in the Age of Shakespeare*. Princeton: Princeton University Press, 1957.

Robin P. Ansell. *Animal Lore in English Literature*. London: Macmillan, 1932.

Schelling, Felix. *The English Chronicle Play*. New York: Macmillan, 1932.

Schoenbaum, Samuel. "Internal Evidence and the Attribution of Elizabethan Plays." *Bulletin of N.Y. Public Library*, 65 (1961), 102-24.

Shakespeare, William. *King Lear*. Ed. Kenneth Muir. The Arden Shakespeare. Cambridge, Mass.: Vintage Books, 1959.

-------. *Measure for Measure*. Ed. J.W. Lever. The Arden Shakespeare. London: Methuen and Co., 1965.

Shakespeare's Library. Ed. W.C. Hazlitt. 2nd ed. London: Reeves and Turner, 1895. VI, 305-387.

Sisson, C.J. "The Laws of Elizabethan Copyright: The Stationers' View." *Library*, 15 (1960). 8-20.

Six Old Plays. Ed. George Steevens. London: S. Leacroft, 1779. II, 377-464.

Spenser, Edmund. *The Faerie Queene*. Ed. J.C. Smith, 2 vols. Oxford: Clarendon Press, 1961.

Stopes, C.C. *The Third Earl of Southampton*. London: Routledge and Kegan Paul, 1922.

Symonds, John Addington. *Shakespeare's Predecessors in the English Drama*. London: Smith Elder, 1884.

Theobald, Lewis. *The Works of Shakespeare*. London: J. Browne, 1733.

Tilley, Morris Palmer. *A Dictionary of the Proverbs in England in the Sixteenth and Seventeenth Centuries*. Ann Arbor: University of Michigan Press, 1950.

Turner, Robert K. Jr. "The Composition of The Insatiate Countess." *Studies in Bibliography*, 12 (1959), 198-203.

Ward, Adolphus W. *History of English Dramatic Literature*. London: Macmillan and Co., 1875.

Wells, Henry W. *A Chronological List of Extant Plays Produced in or about London*, 1581-1642. New York: Columbia University Press, 1940.

William Shakespeare: The Complete Works. Ed. Alfred Harbage. Baltimore: Penguin Books, 1969.

Williams, George W. "Setting by Formes in Quarto Printing." *Studies in Bibliography*, 11 (1958), 39-53.

Wright, Louis B. *Middle-Class Culture in Elizabethan England*. Chapel Hill: University of North Carolina Press, 1935.

Young, Robert. *Analytical Concordance to the Holy Bible*. 8th edition. London: Lutterworth Press, 1961.